WEDNESDAY HOLMES

YOU DESERVE THE WHOLE WORLD

HarperCollins*Publishers*

www.harpercollins.co.uk

HarperCollinsPublishers
Macken House, 39/40 Mayor Street Upper
Dublin 1, DO1 C9W8, Ireland

First published by HarperCollinsPublishers 2023

1 3 5 7 9 10 8 6 4 2

A catalogue record of this book is available from the British Library

ISBN 978-0-00-860681-7

Printed and bound by PNB, Latvia

MIX
Paper | Supporting
responsible forestry
FSC™ C007454

This book is produced from independently certified FSC™ paper to
ensure responsible forest management.

For more information visit: www.harpercollins.co.uk/green

CONTENTS

INTRODUCTION

When I was younger, I felt like my life had no direction. I didn't know if I would survive my teenagehood. Maybe many people have felt the same.

So when I picked up my pen to create this book, I thought, 'I need to create the book I needed when I was younger.'

I hope that through these words and artworks, I can implore you to see how much light you have inside of you. I hope that through this book, you can be reminded that life is not only worth living, but that it can be a wonderful experience too.

The world is a challenging place – this isn't a secret. I'm hoping you will leave this book's journey feeling more energised to take on the whole universe.

WEDNESDAYxx

SELF-BELIEF

KEEP SHINING YOUR WAY
THROUGH THE DARK,
BECAUSE YOU HAVE NO IDEA
WHO MIGHT BE FOLLOWING
YOUR LIGHT
IN SEARCH OF PEACE

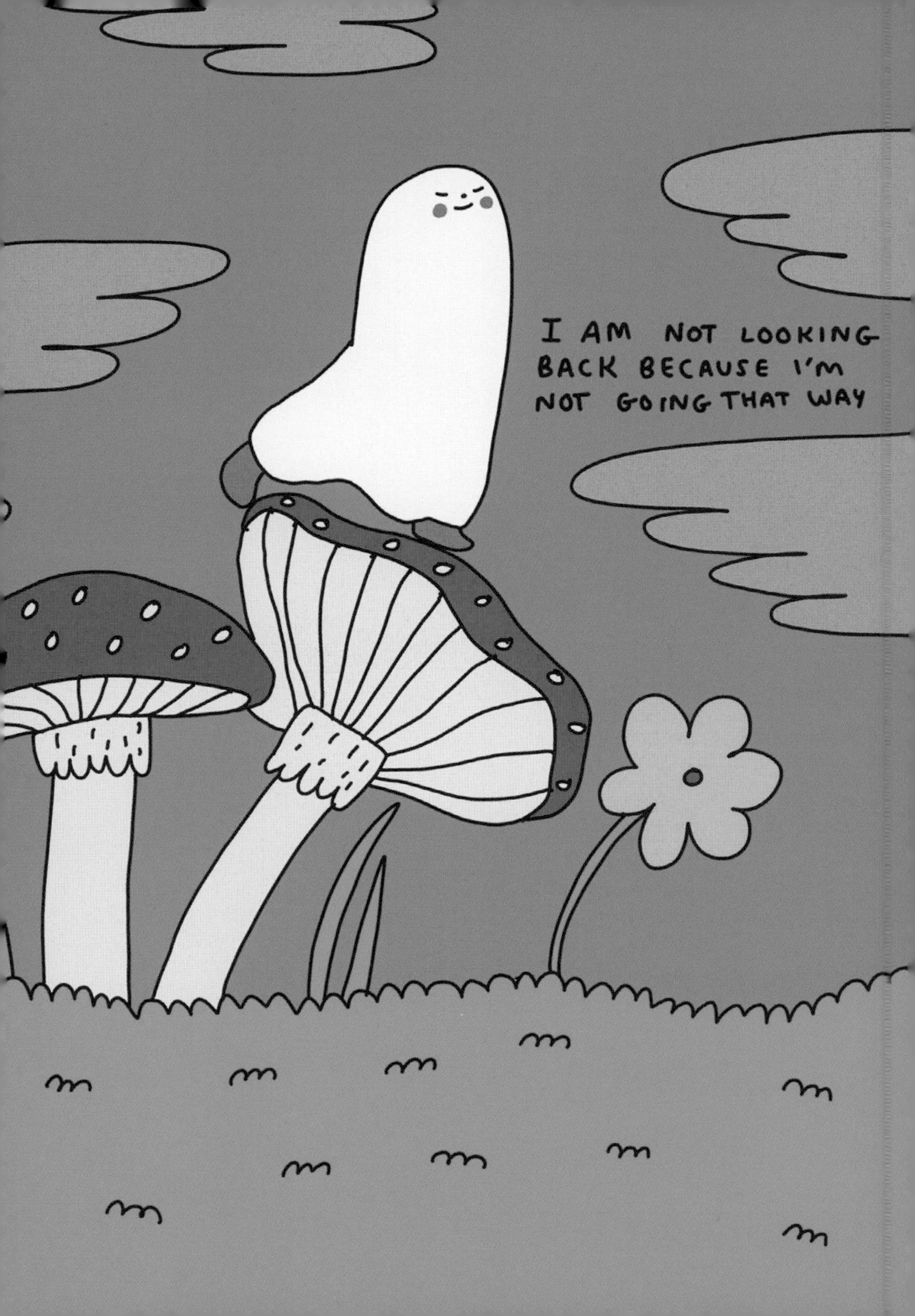
I AM NOT LOOKING BACK BECAUSE I'M NOT GOING THAT WAY

This journey is going to
challenge you. But in it all,
do not forget that you are
worthy of everything
you dream of.

Believe that you are the
magic you seek. You are the
light in the dark.

And when the journey leads
you back to yourself, you will
realise that you were always
on the right path.

Here's to the moments of
strength and softness.

Here's to the moments that
remind us we are human.

Here's to the moments of
serenity and peace.

Here's to the moments
that remind us we are
worthy of light.

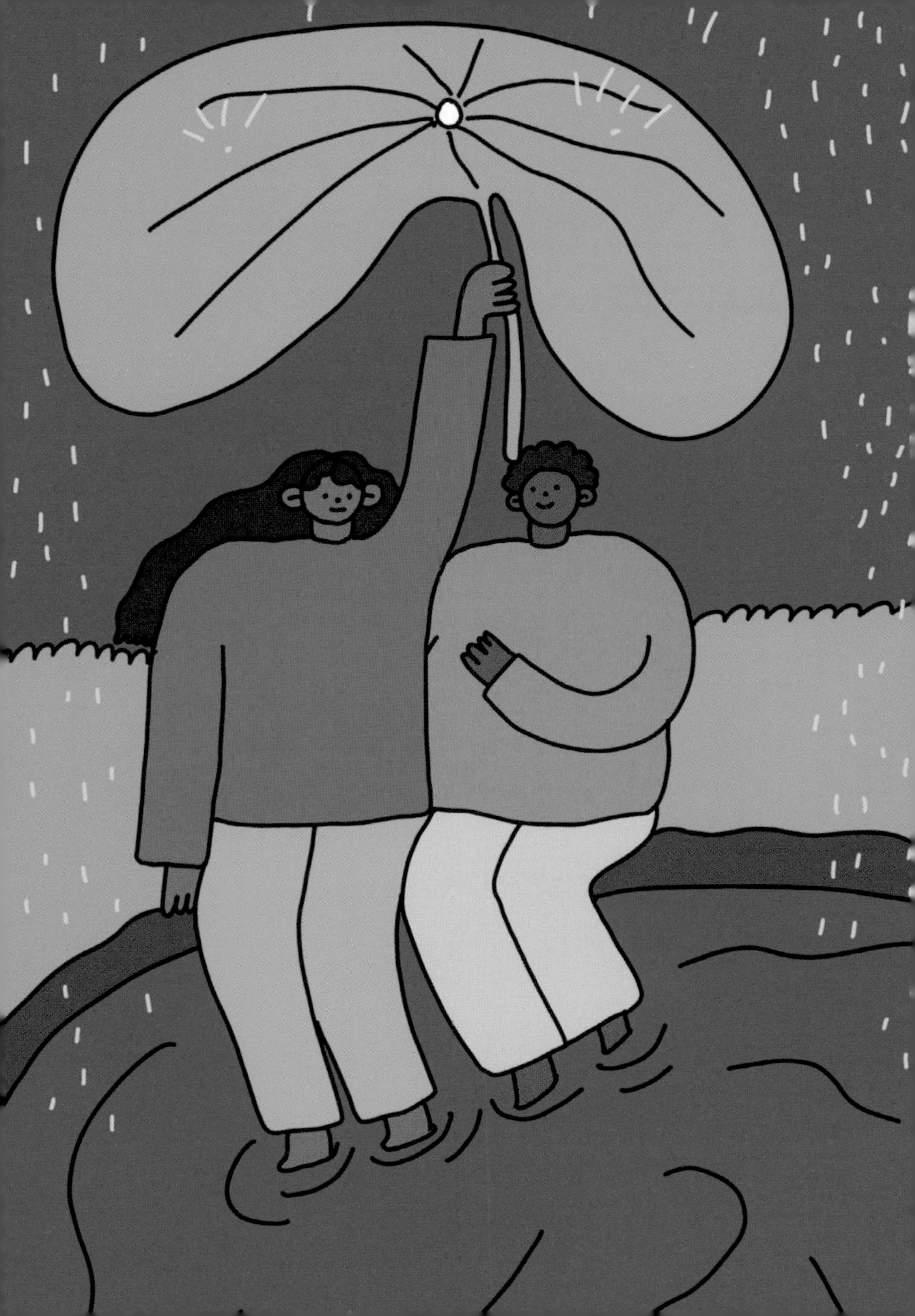

When you lie down tonight,
remember that you did the
best you could today.

You're a miracle to behold.

You're more than enough.

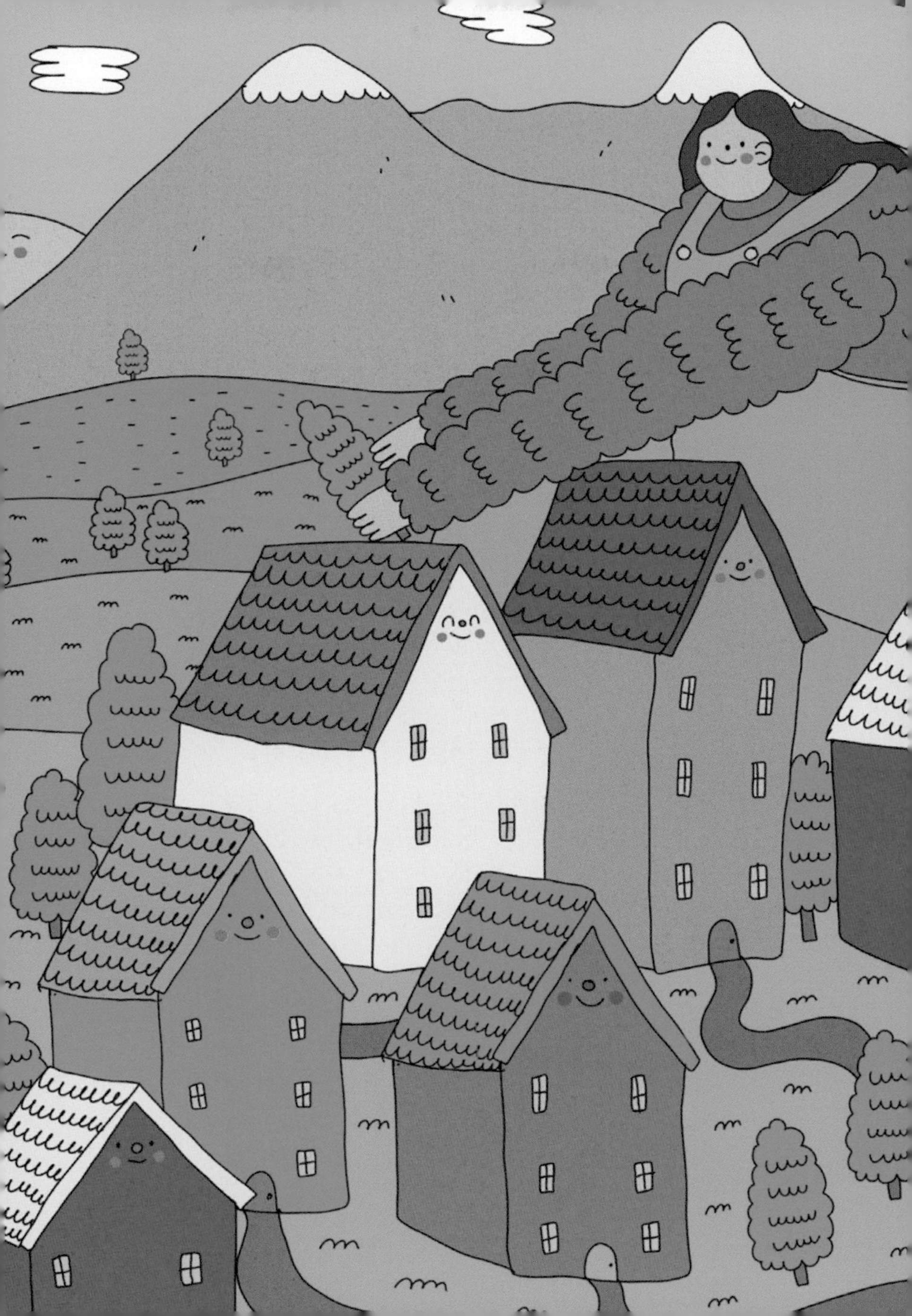

You are the vast expanse
of the sky.

You are the river running
free and wild.

You are the veins of the earth,
holy mycelium.

You are the light and the
warmth of the sun.

You are never ending.

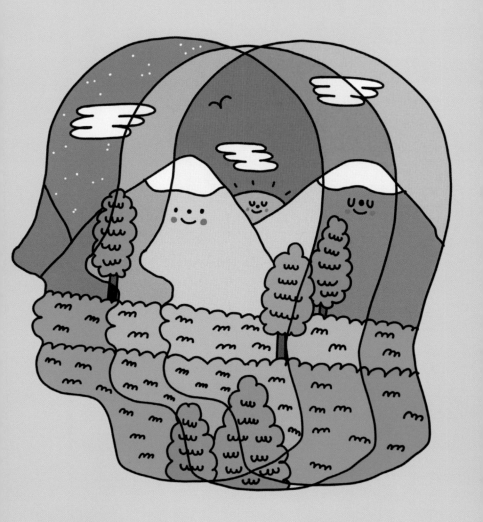

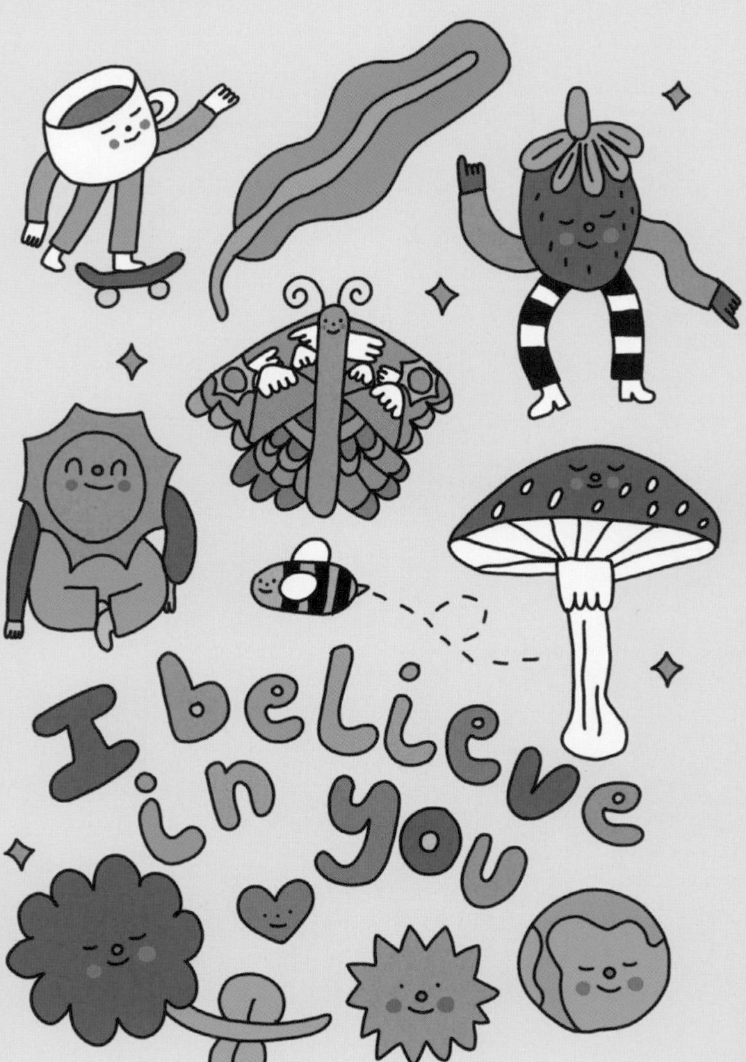
I believe in you

Look how far you have
made it. You are such a force
of nature and you don't
even realise it.

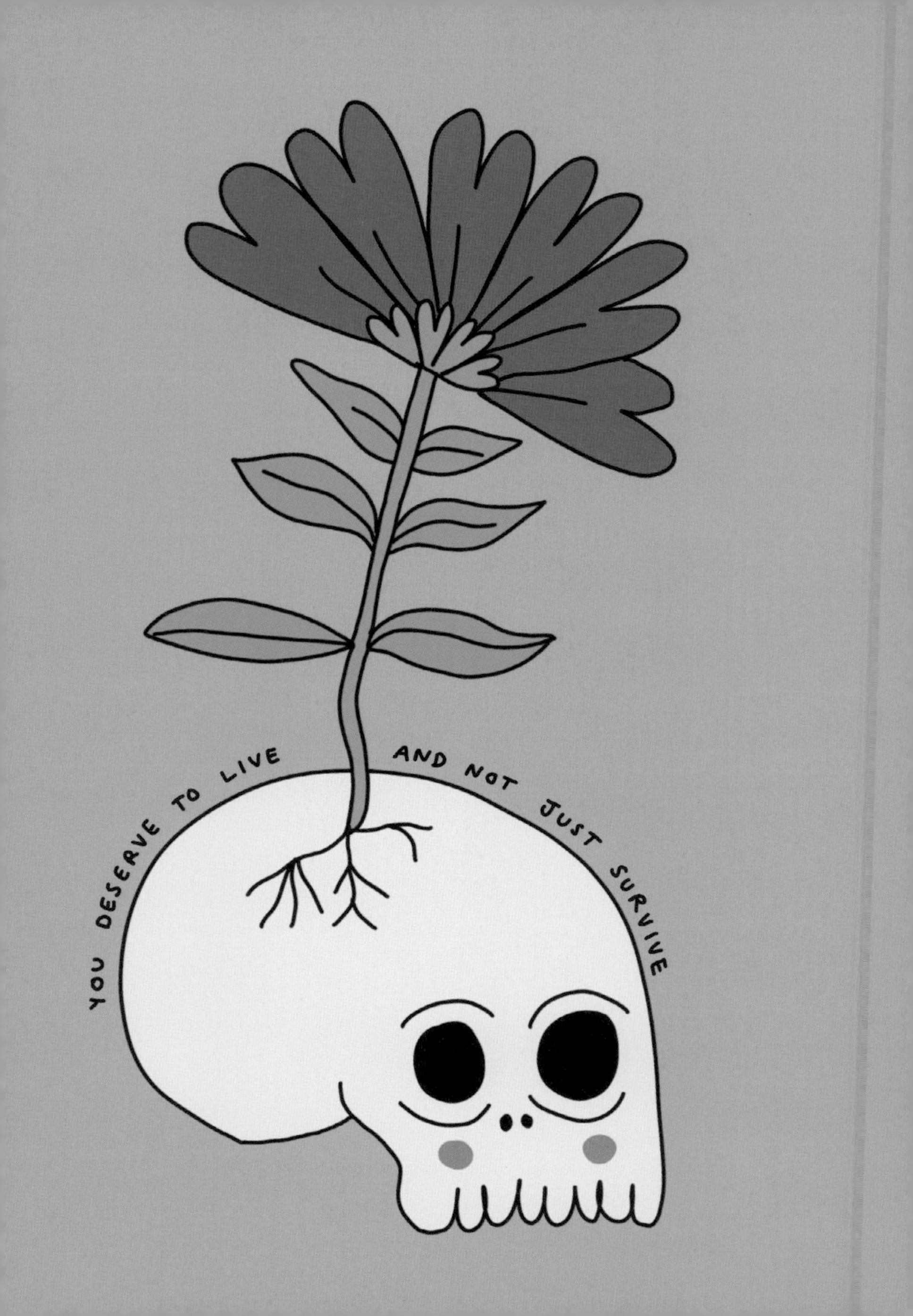
YOU DESERVE TO LIVE
AND NOT JUST SURVIVE

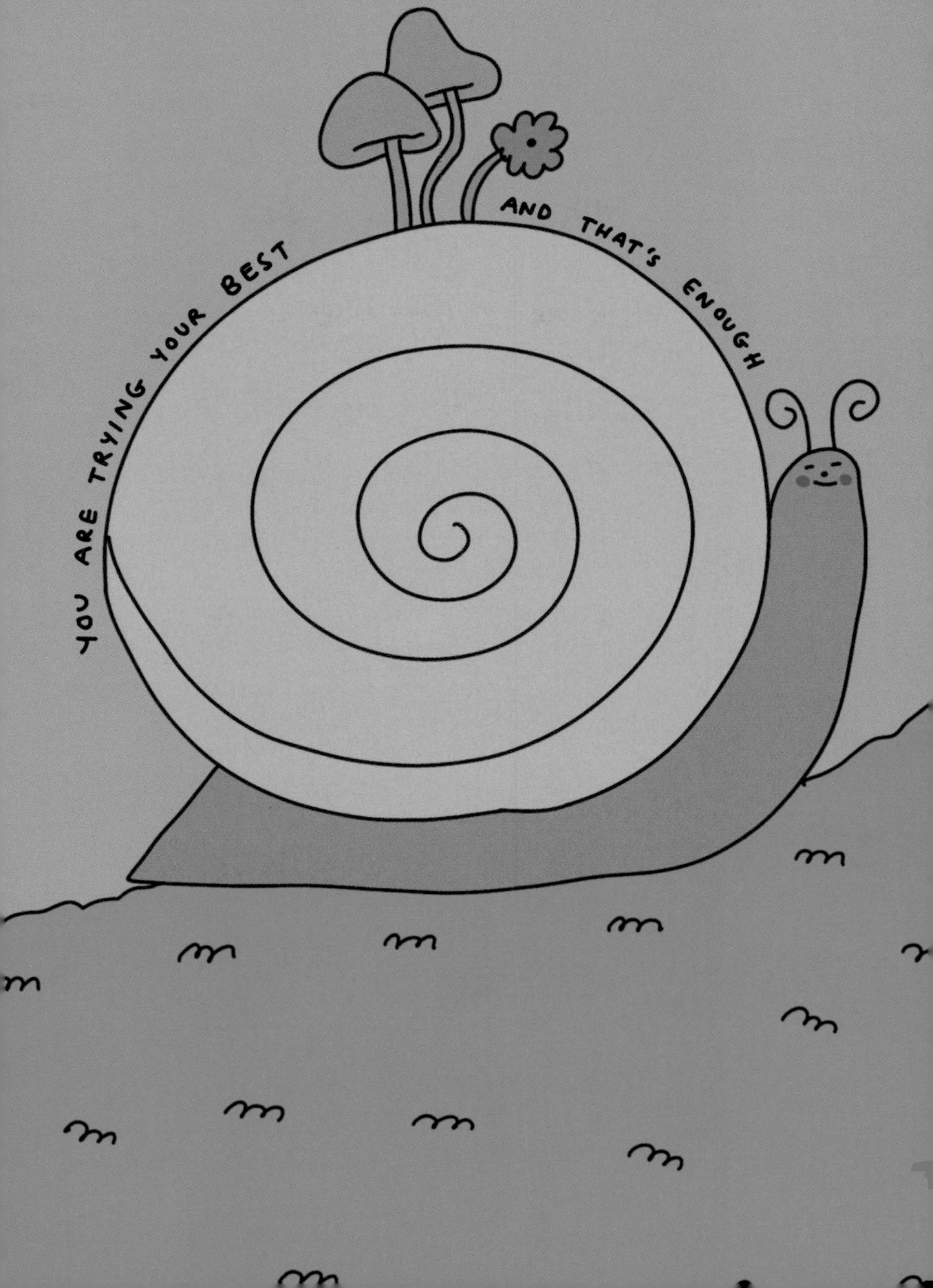
YOU ARE TRYING YOUR BEST
AND THAT'S ENOUGH

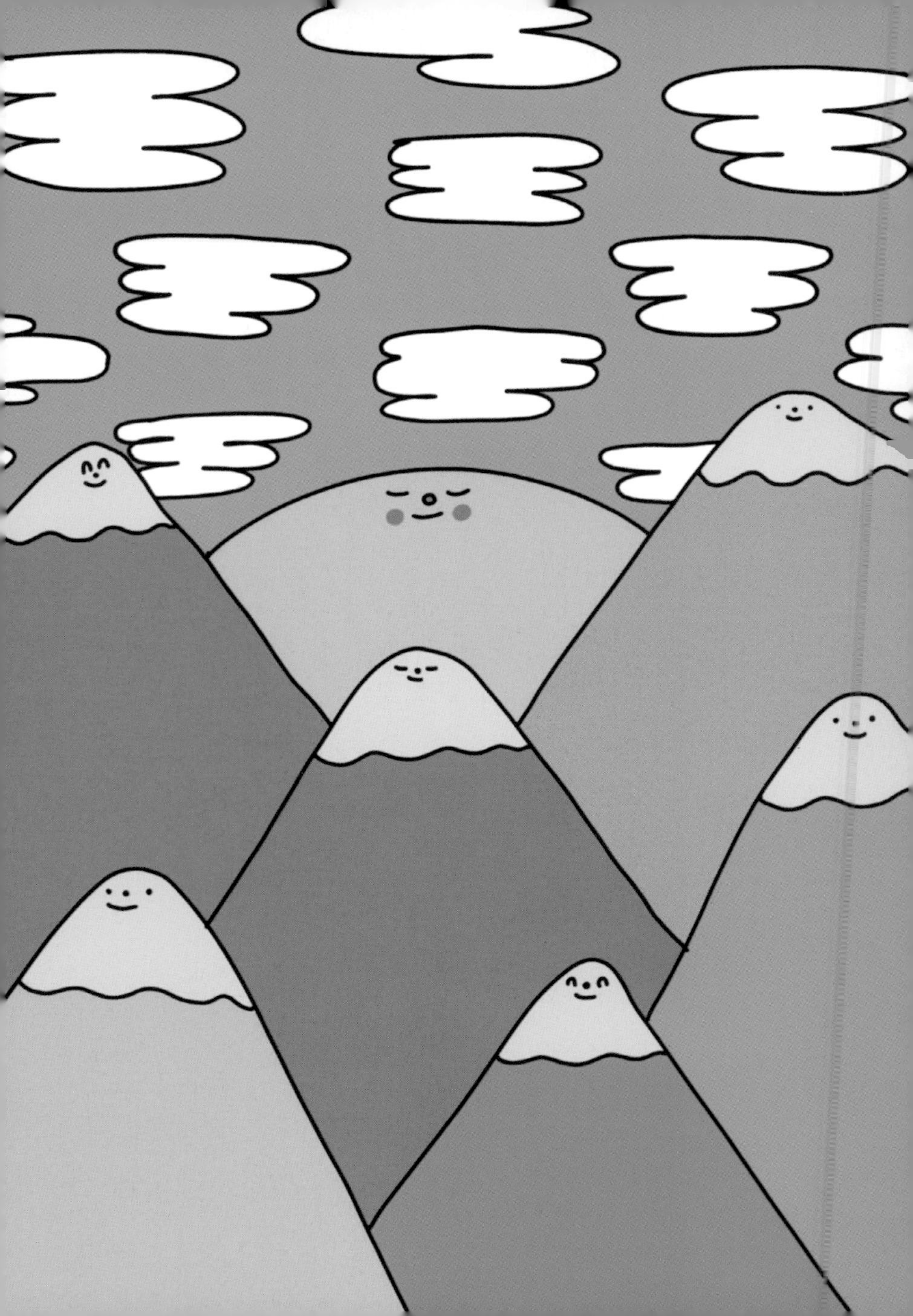

It's good to see you move
mountains for your
own happiness.

It's good to know you realise
how worthy you are.

21

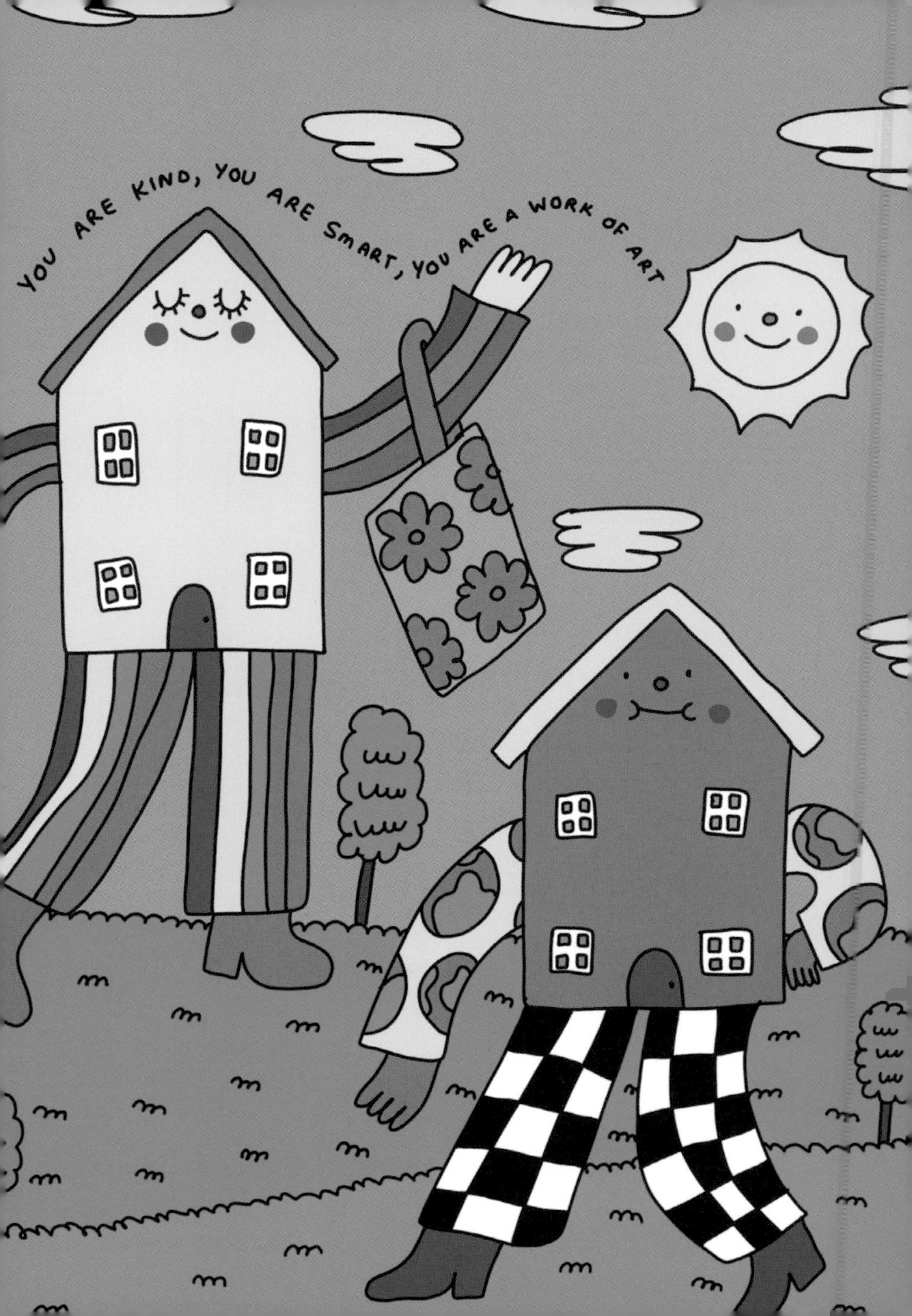
YOU ARE KIND, YOU ARE SMART, YOU ARE A WORK OF ART

Everything you need
is already within you.

It was always you.

The magic was you.

The softness and strength
were always you.

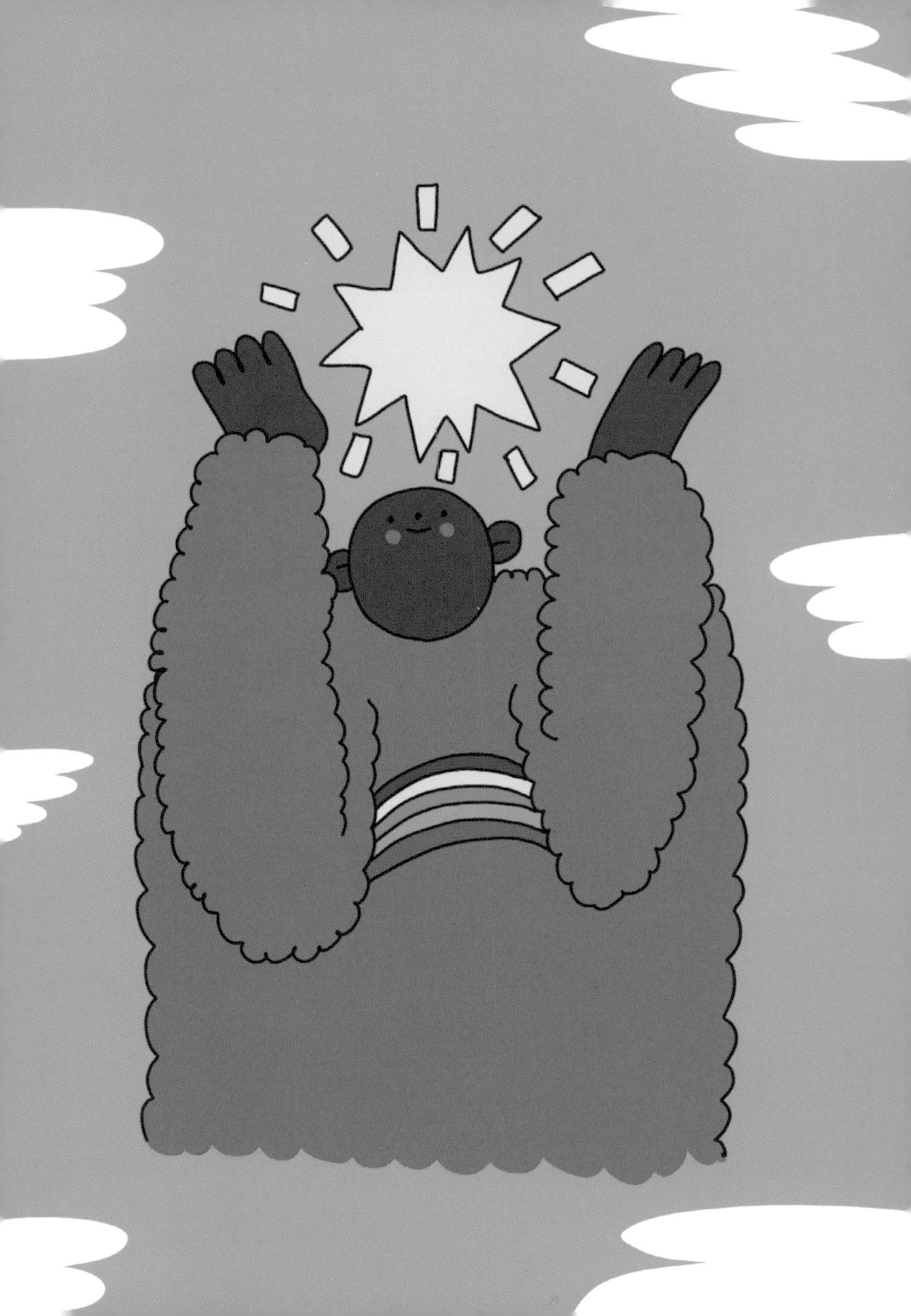

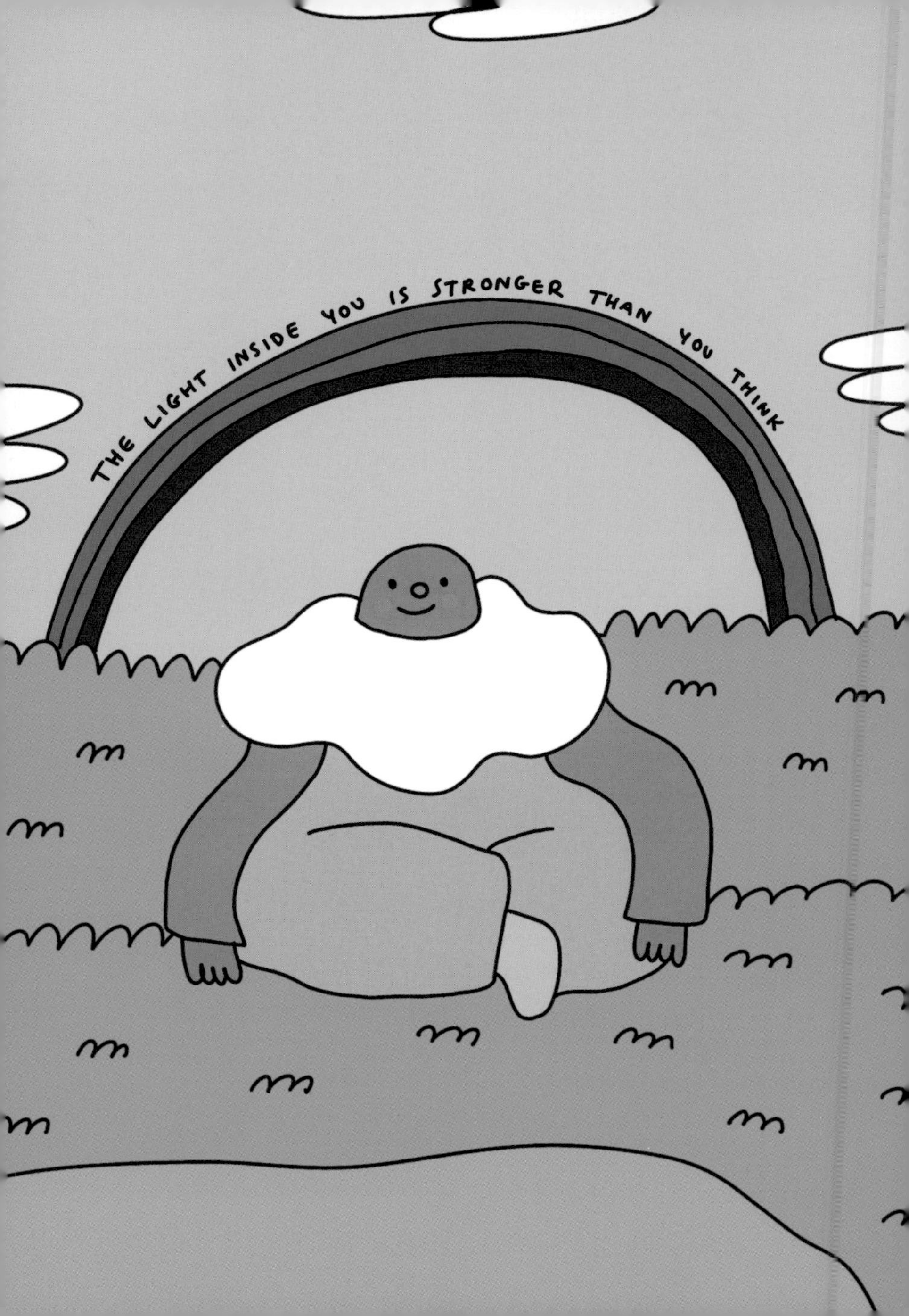
THE LIGHT INSIDE YOU IS STRONGER THAN YOU THINK

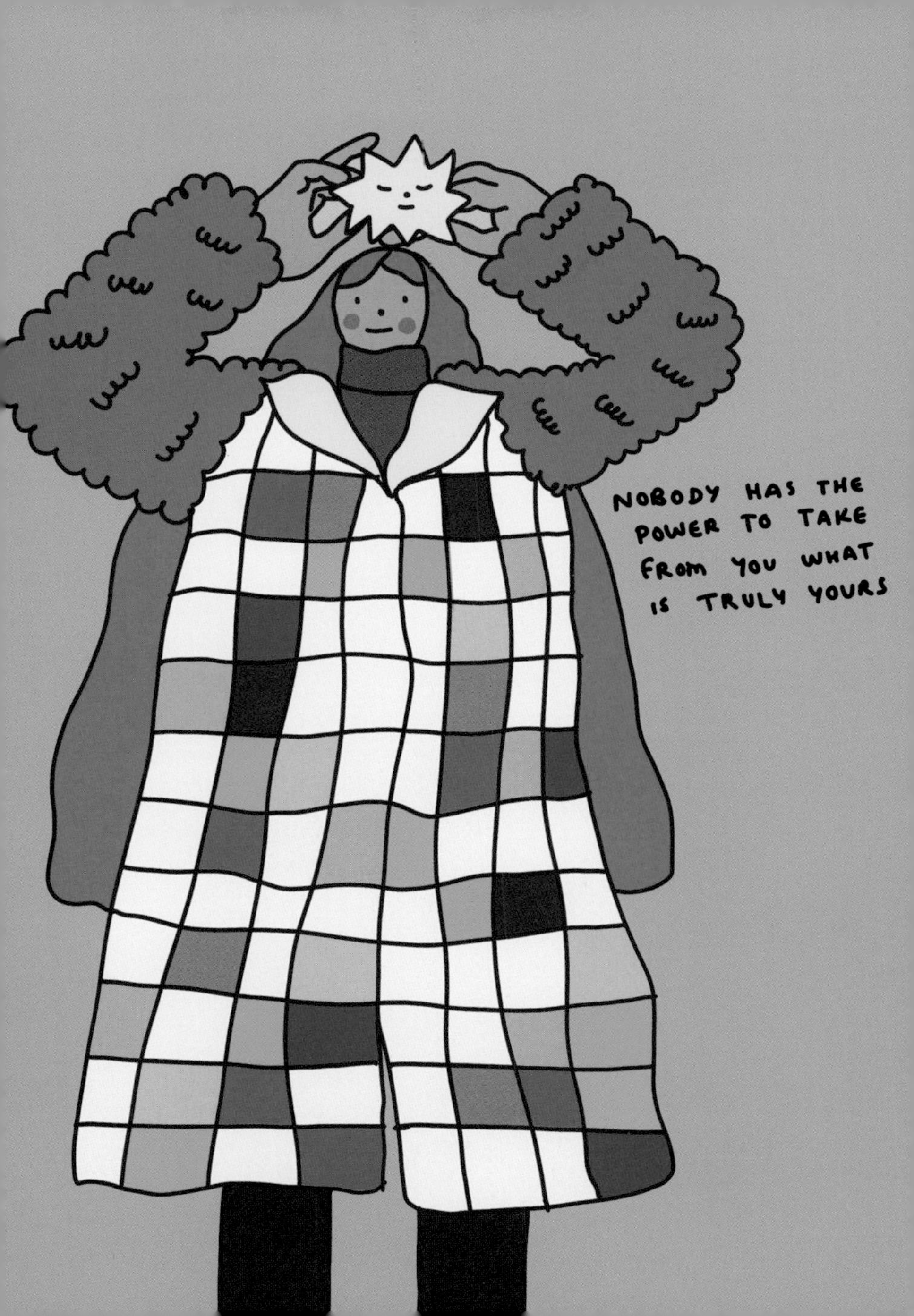

NOBODY HAS THE
POWER TO TAKE
FROM YOU WHAT
IS TRULY YOURS

Talk kindly to yourself.

You have to be with yourself
for the rest of your life.
You might as well be
best friends.

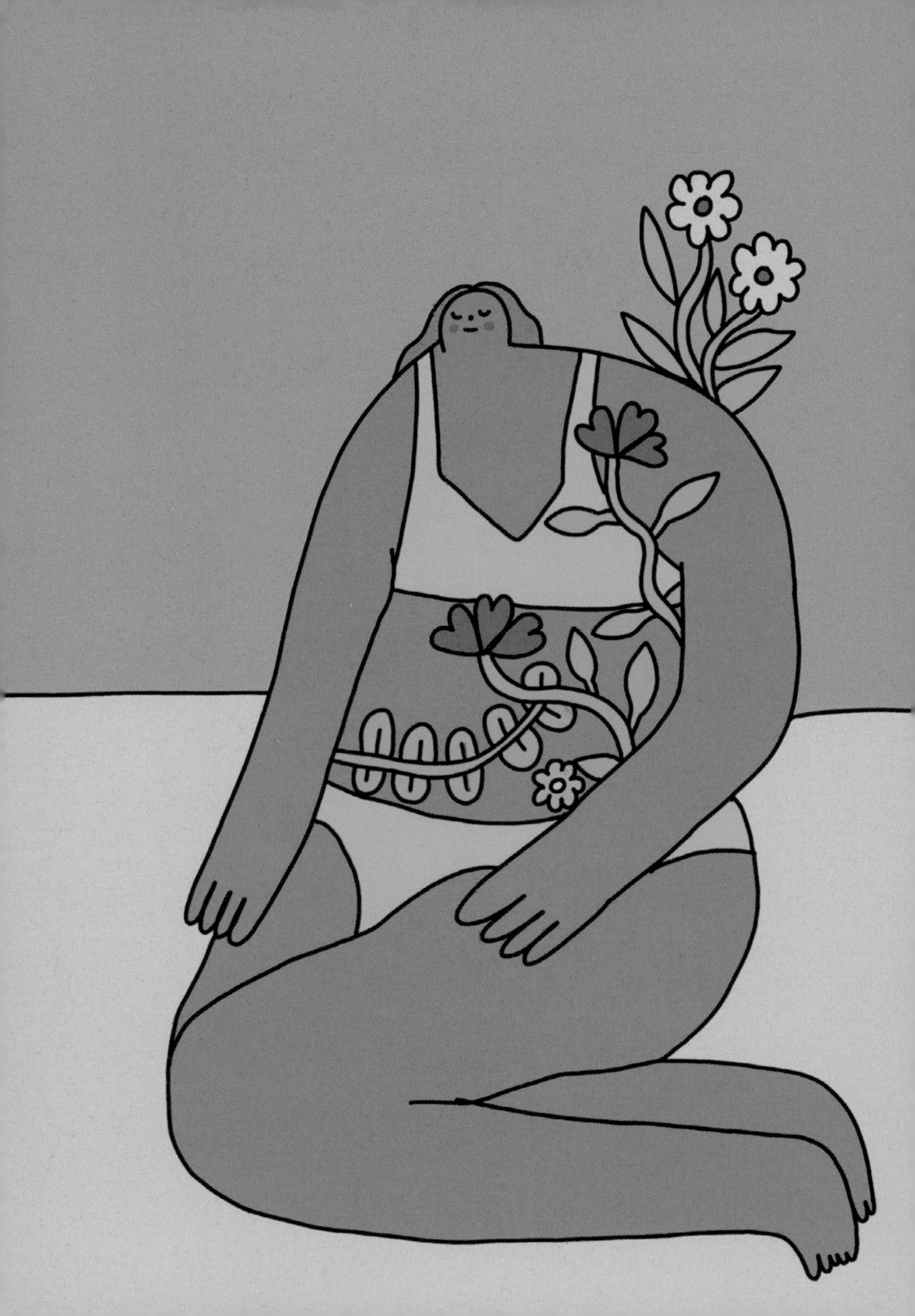

COURAGE

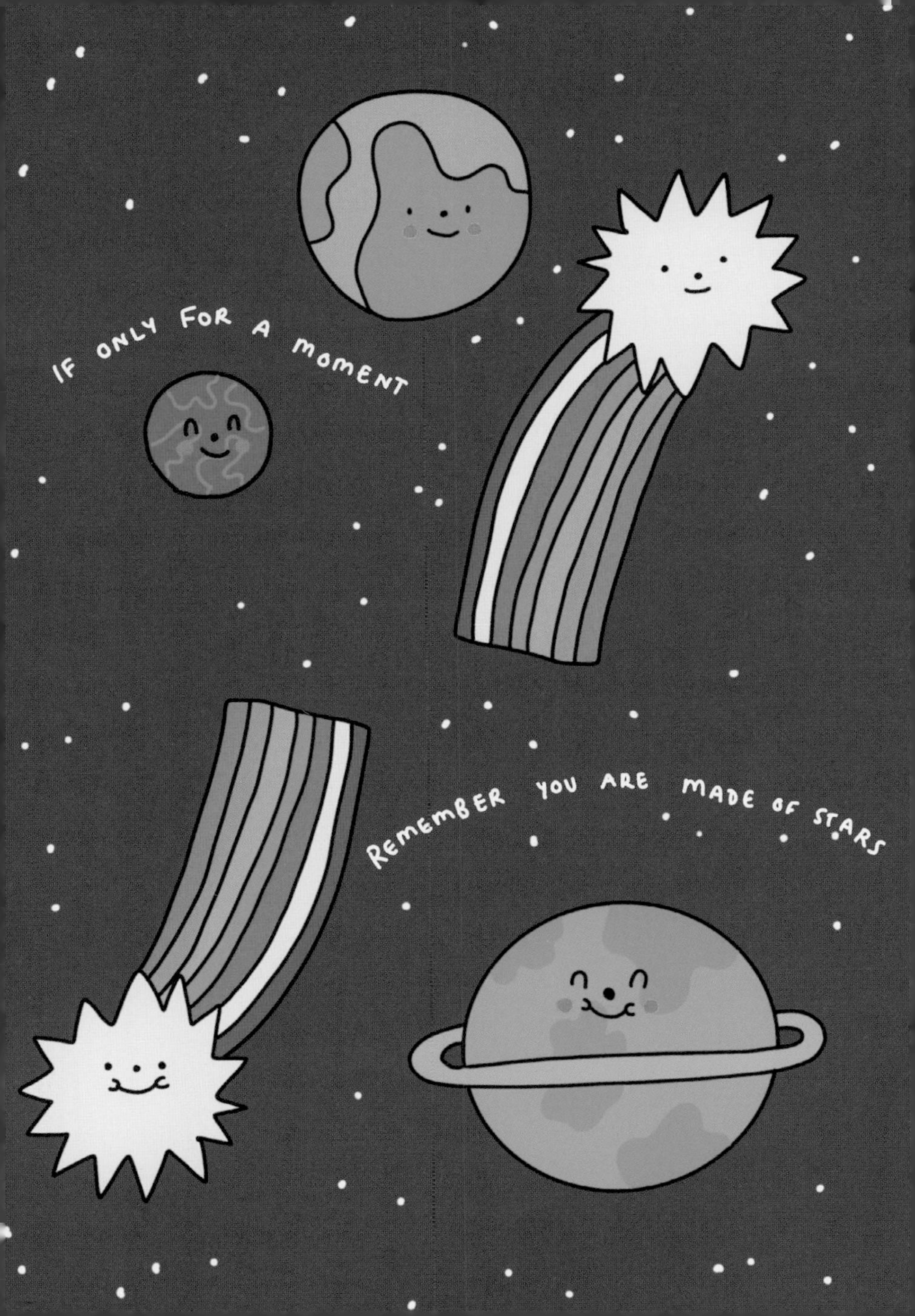
IF ONLY FOR A MOMENT
REMEMBER YOU ARE MADE OF STARS

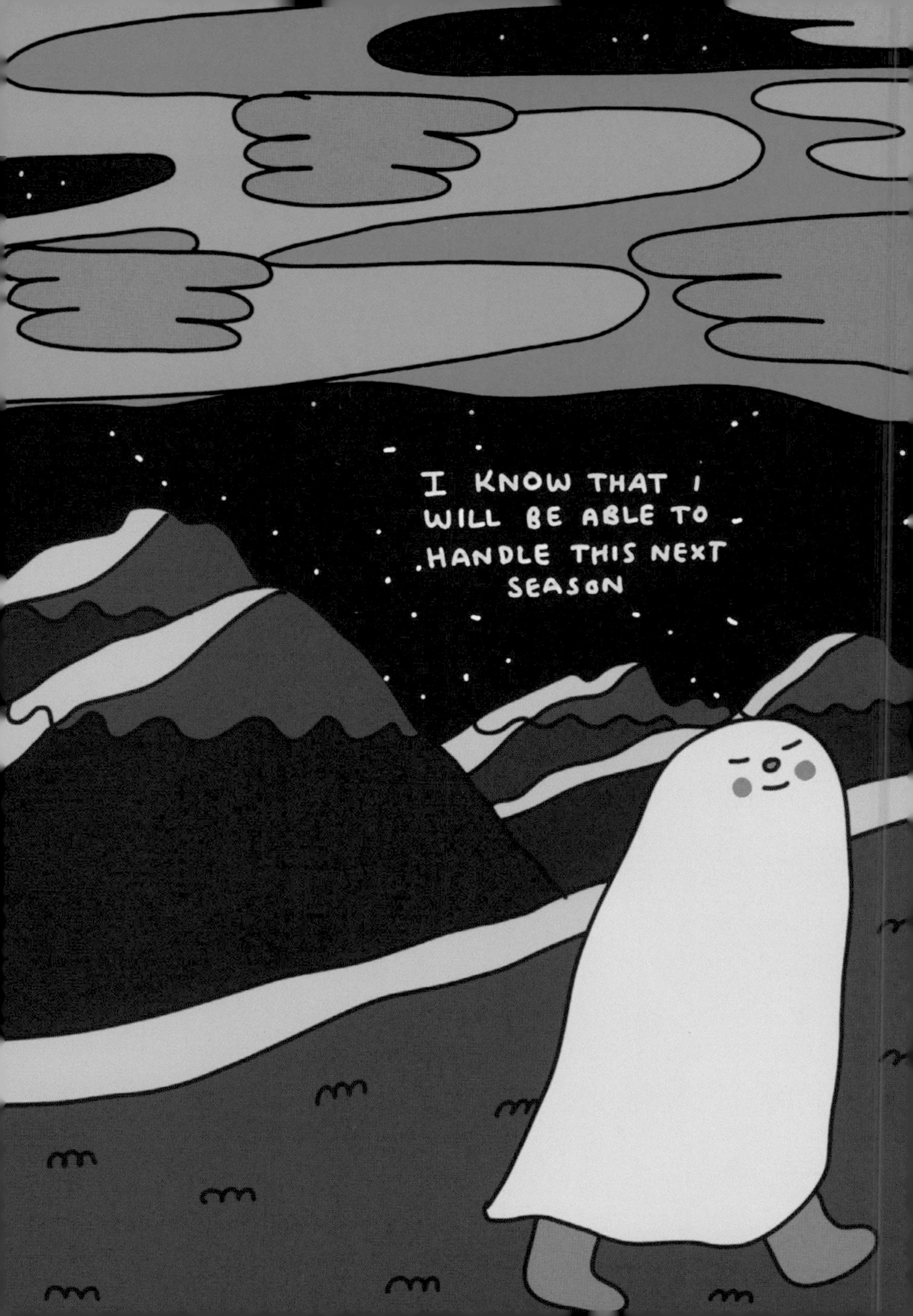
I KNOW THAT I WILL BE ABLE TO HANDLE THIS NEXT SEASON

Don't let the night trick
you into thinking that it
will last for ever.

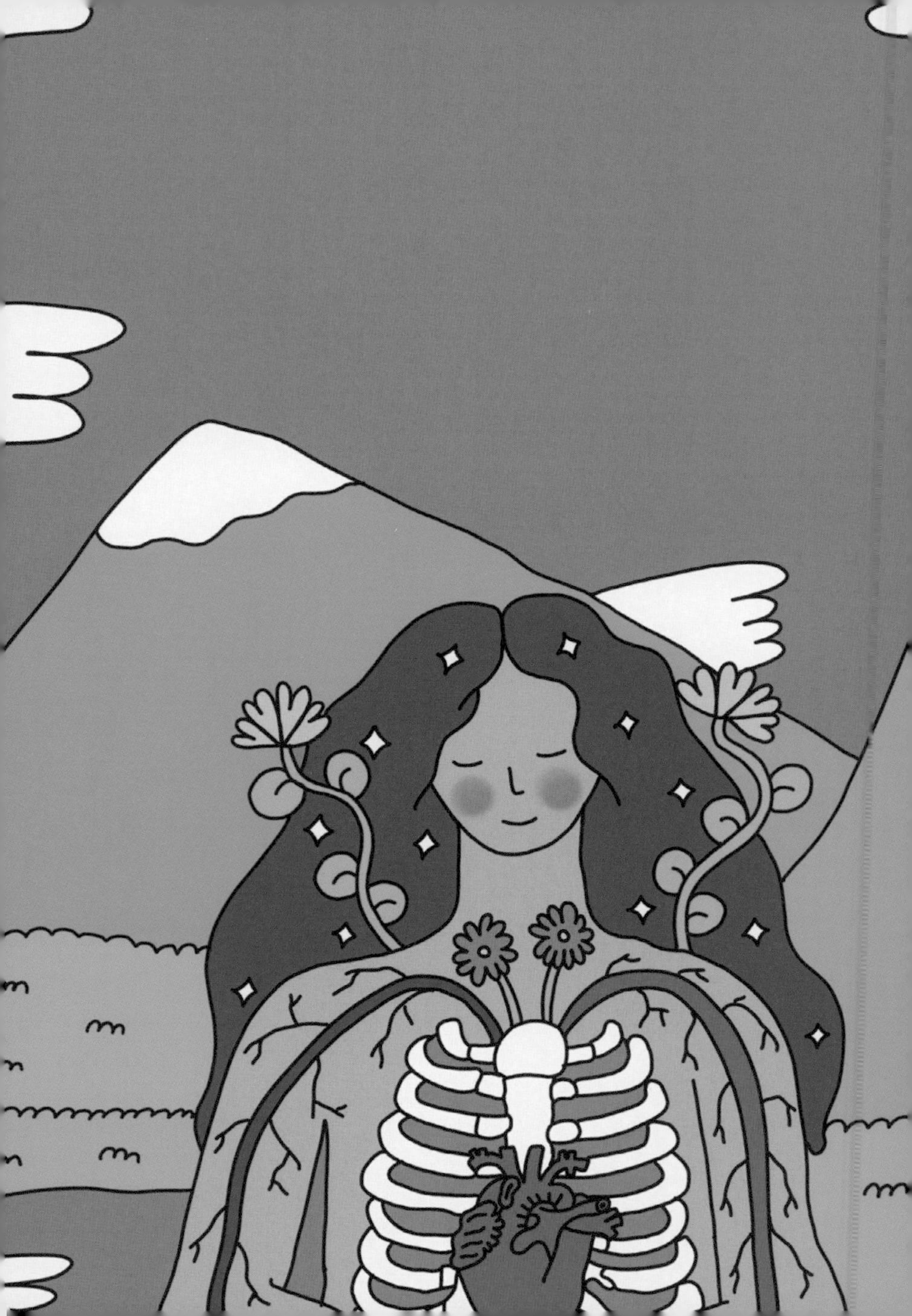

If only you could see
just how magic you are.

Look at you, living each
day in boldness.

Look at you,
shining your light.

Look at you, blooming
in places you dreamed
of blooming.

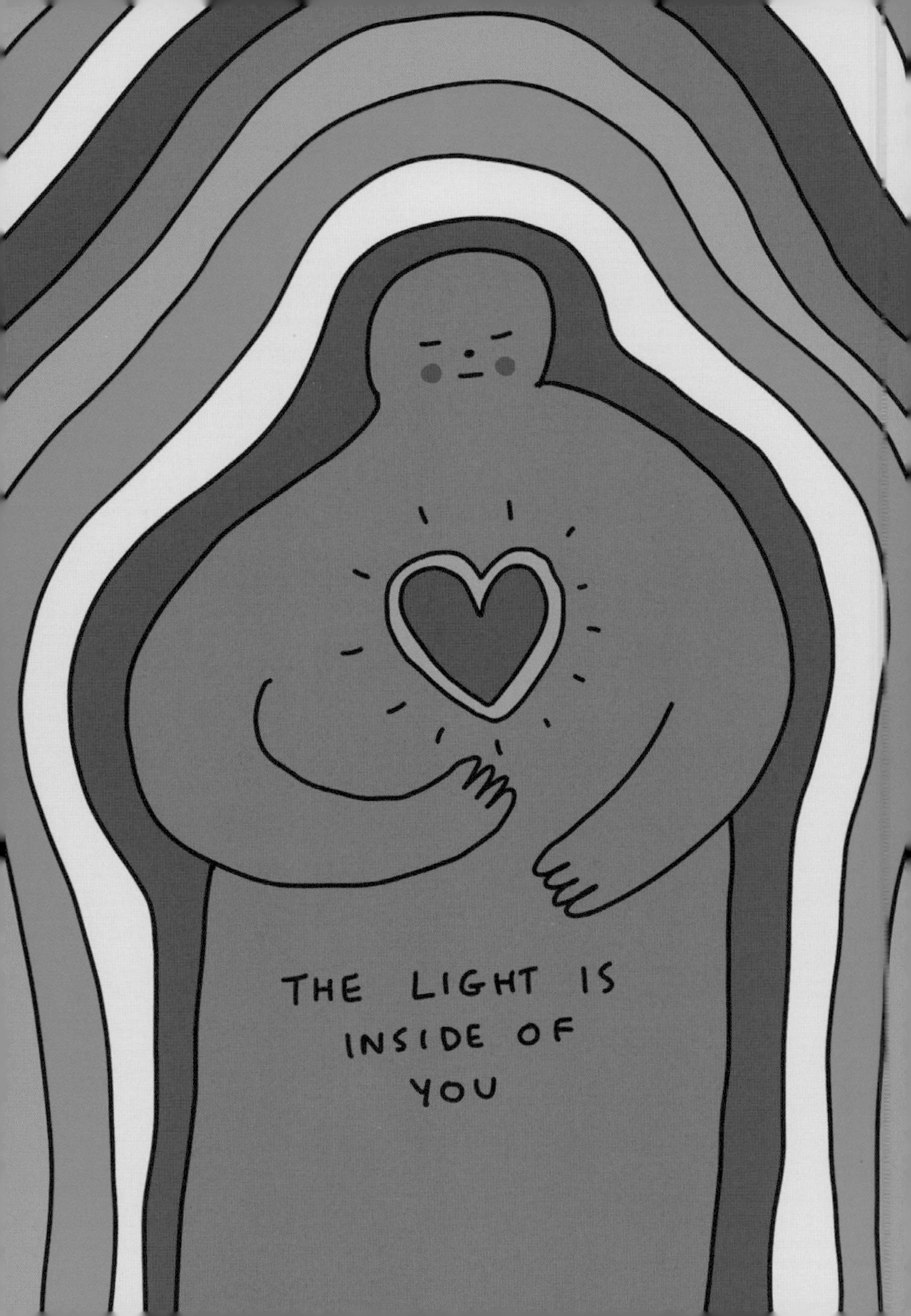
THE LIGHT IS
INSIDE OF
YOU

I see you creating your
own worlds. I see you
conjuring up your own joy.

Believe in your power to make
mountains move.

Believe in your power
to shift dimensions.
Believe in your ability to
make dreams come true.

Witnessing you is a
beauty to behold.

It's OK if you're taking
time to focus on you.
You don't have to be
producing something every
moment of the year. You're
worth so much more than
that. So reclaim your time
without guilt.

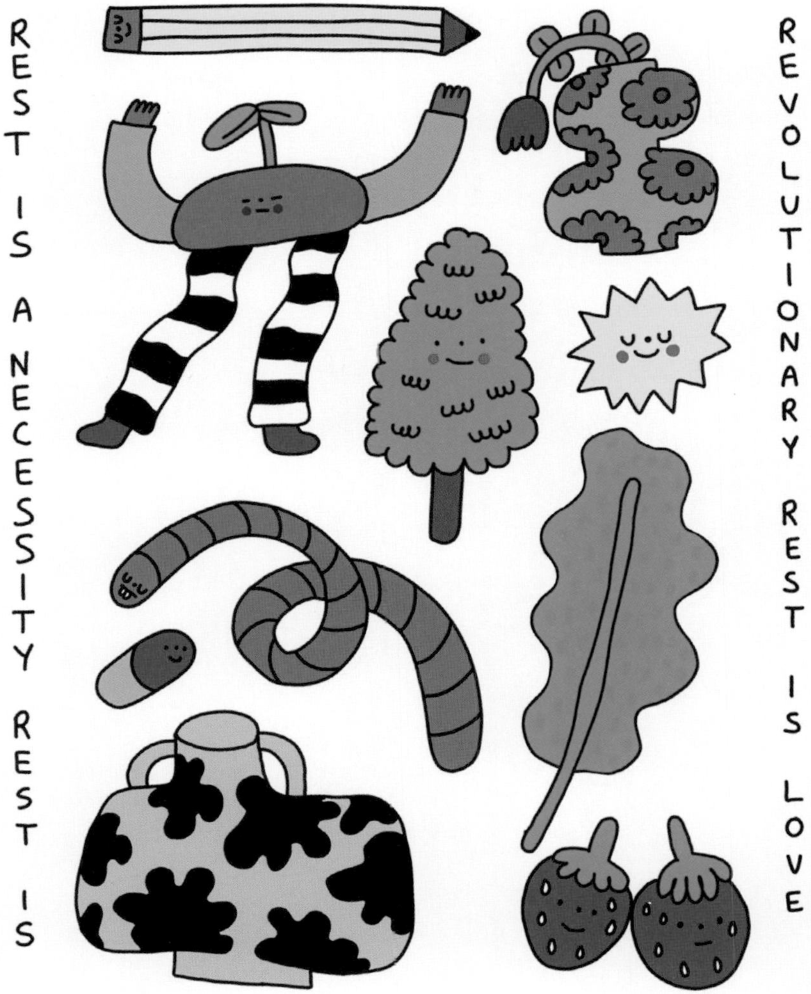
REST IS A NECESSITY REST IS
REVOLUTIONARY REST IS LOVE

Sometimes life can feel hard.
It's hard to wake up.
It's hard to find a routine.
Know that the hard times will
pass. They, one day, will feel
like a vague memory.

May the good times
come soon. May they bathe
you in their light and show
you that life can also feel
soft and easy.

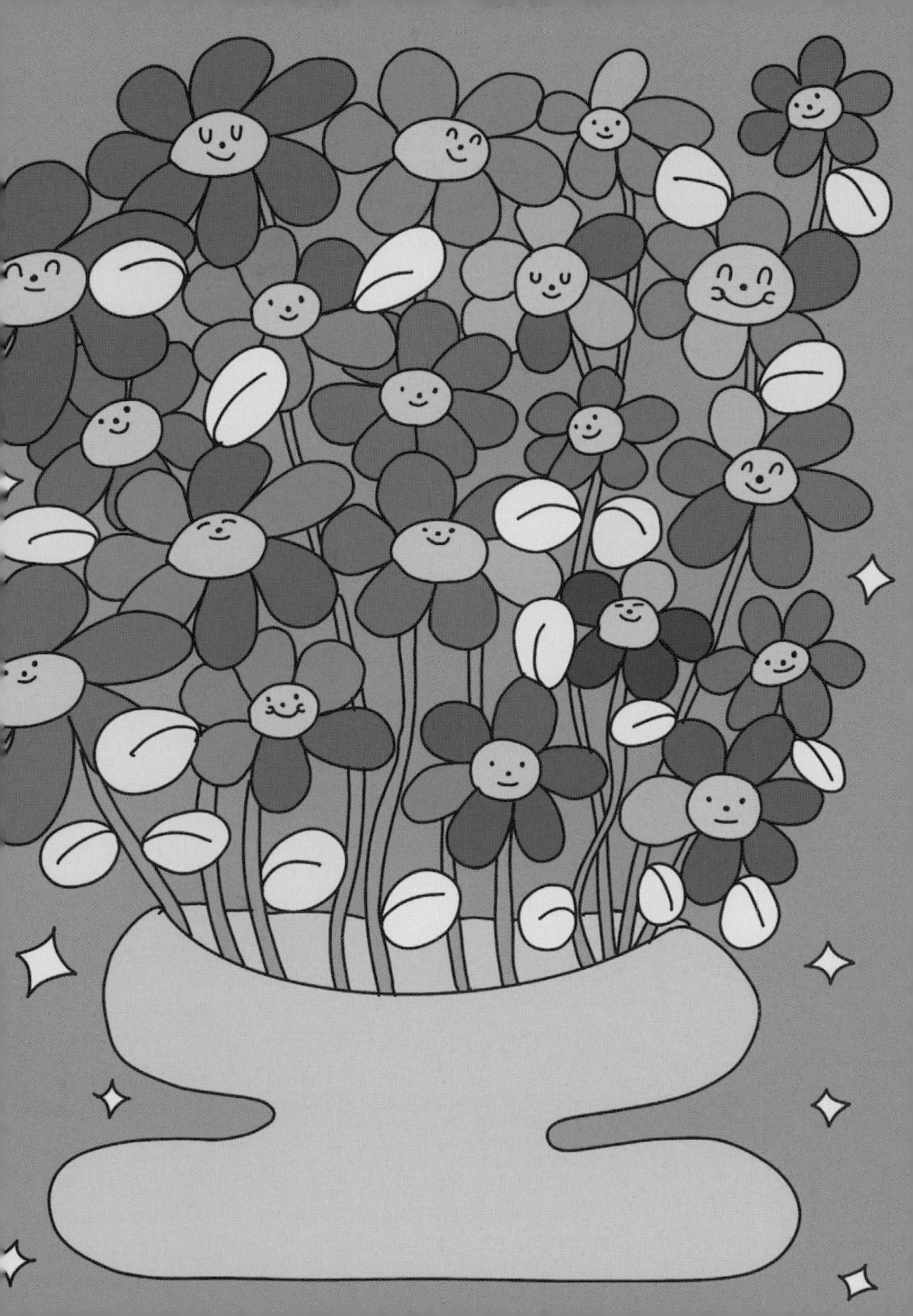

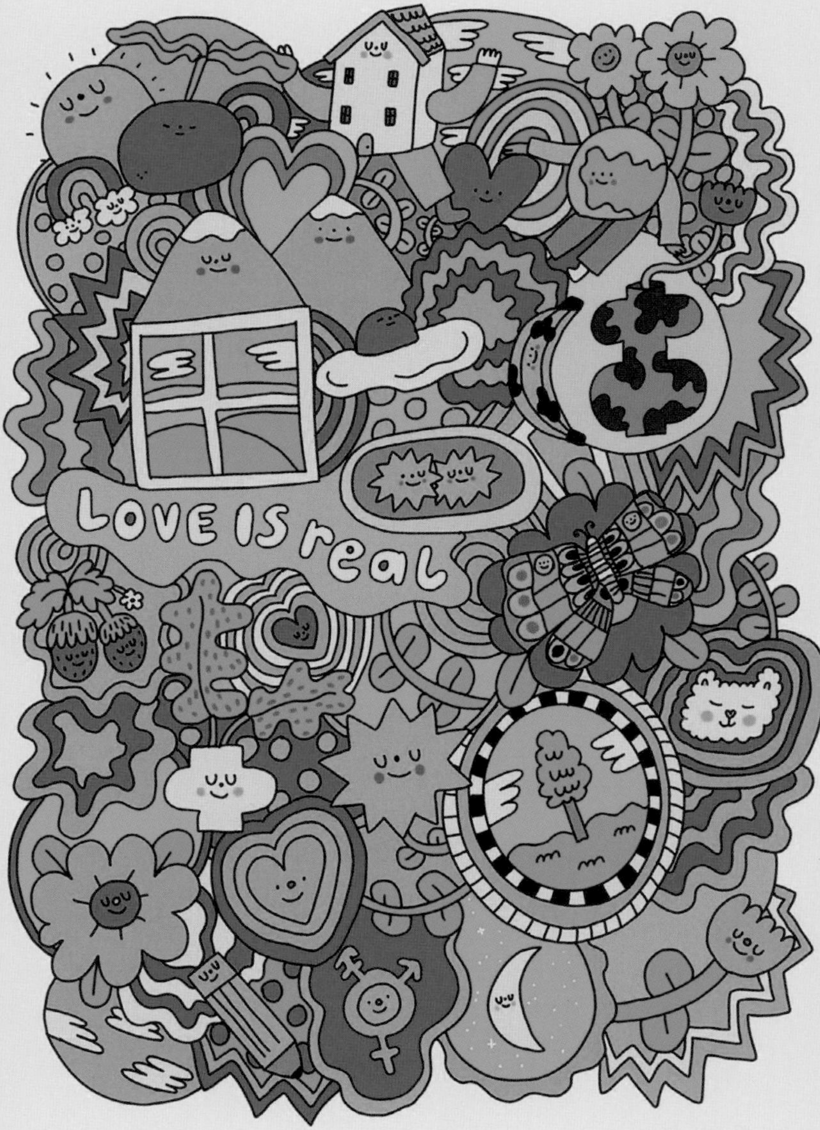
LOVE IS real

I am choosing to believe
that love is real.

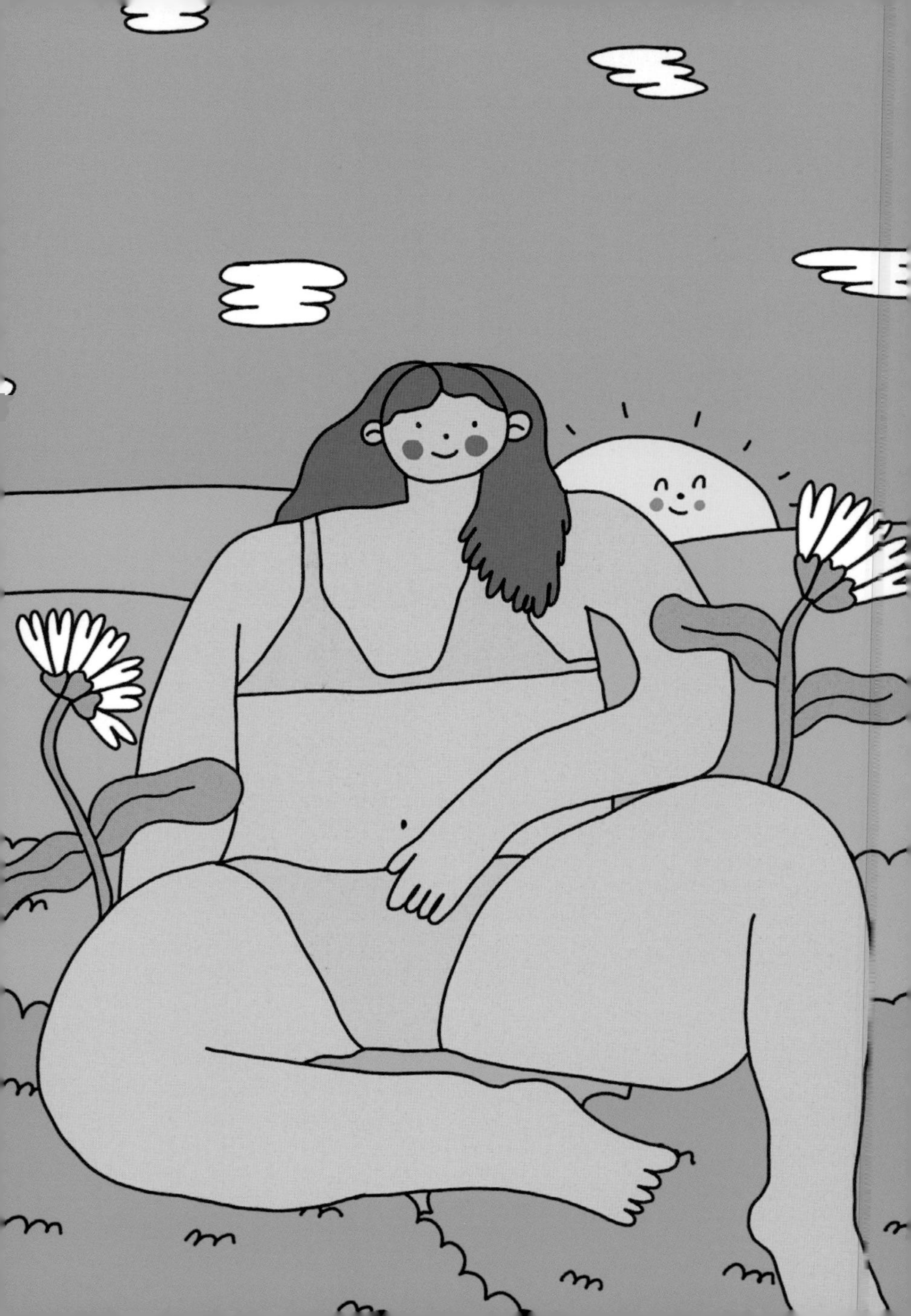

It takes courage to step up
and ask for what you need.
You've travelled so far on this
journey. I'm proud of you.

THERE'S A WHOLE UNIVERSE INSIDE OF YOU

IF YOU'RE LOOKING FOR A SIGN THAT
THIS ALL MEANS SOMETHING, HERE
IT IS

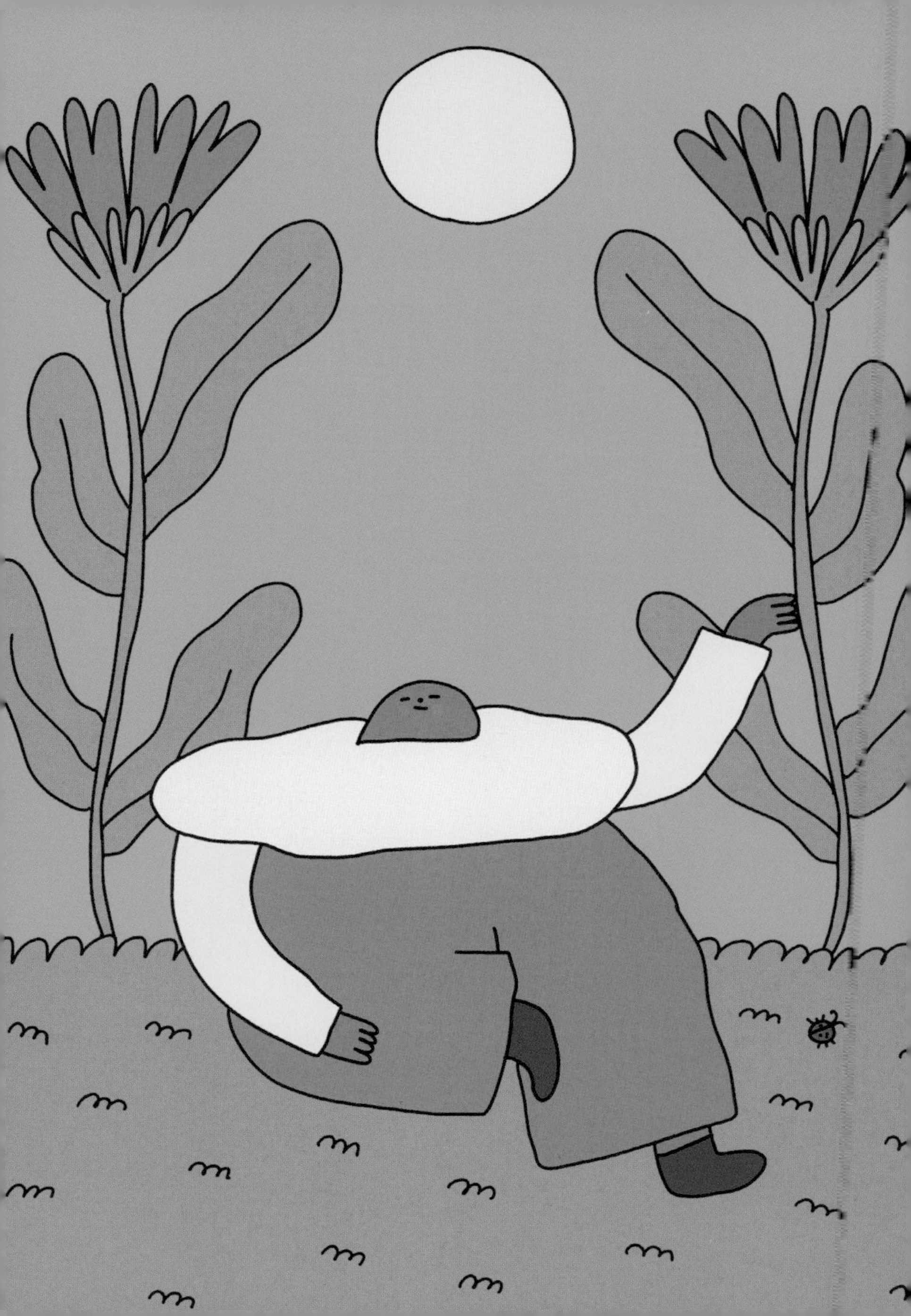

Figure out what you are
destined to hold, and let
the rest free.

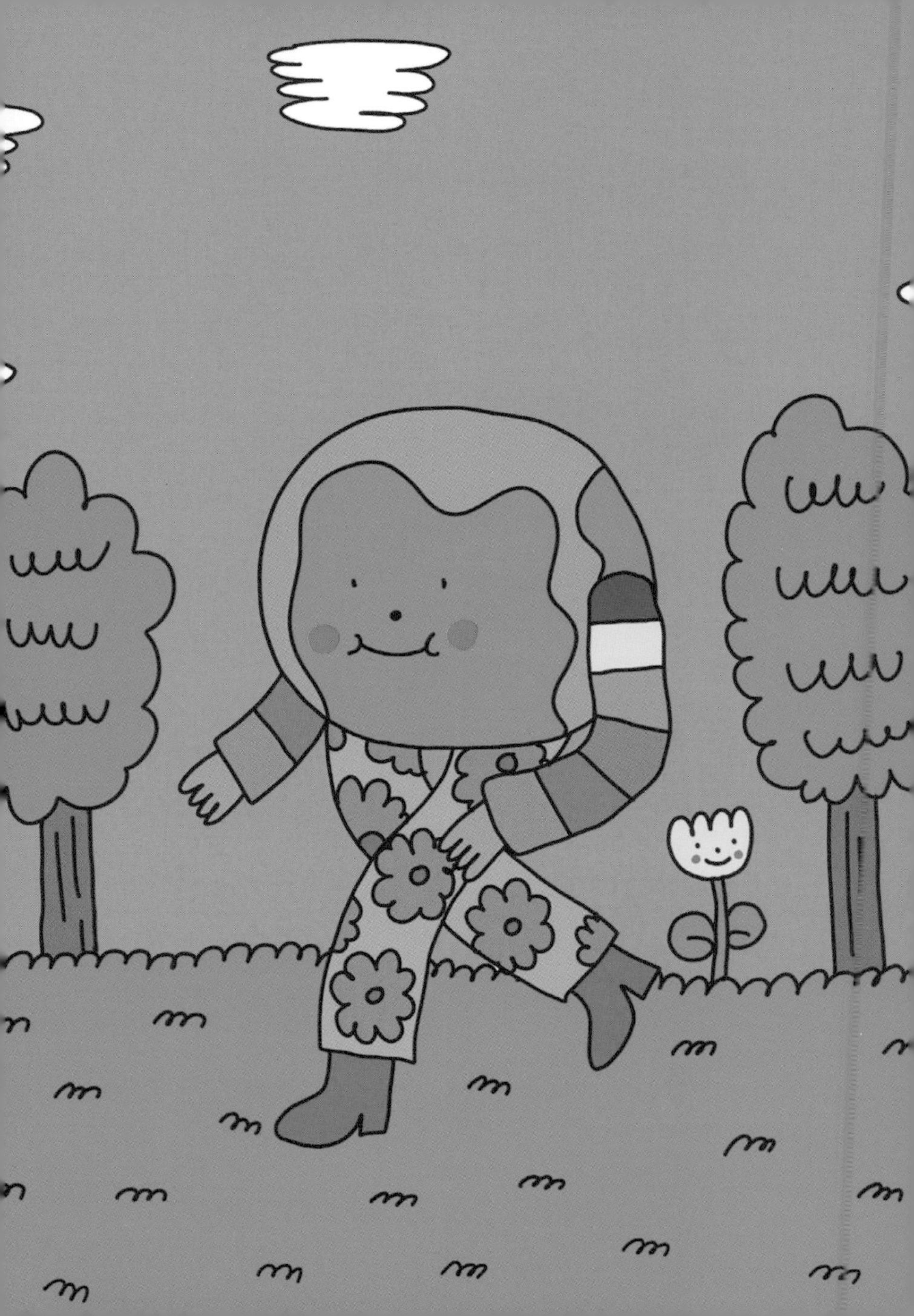

I hope that you get the chance
to heal from the things that
you don't like to talk about.

I see you daring to journey
down this new road.
May you discover that this
path is sweet with flowers.

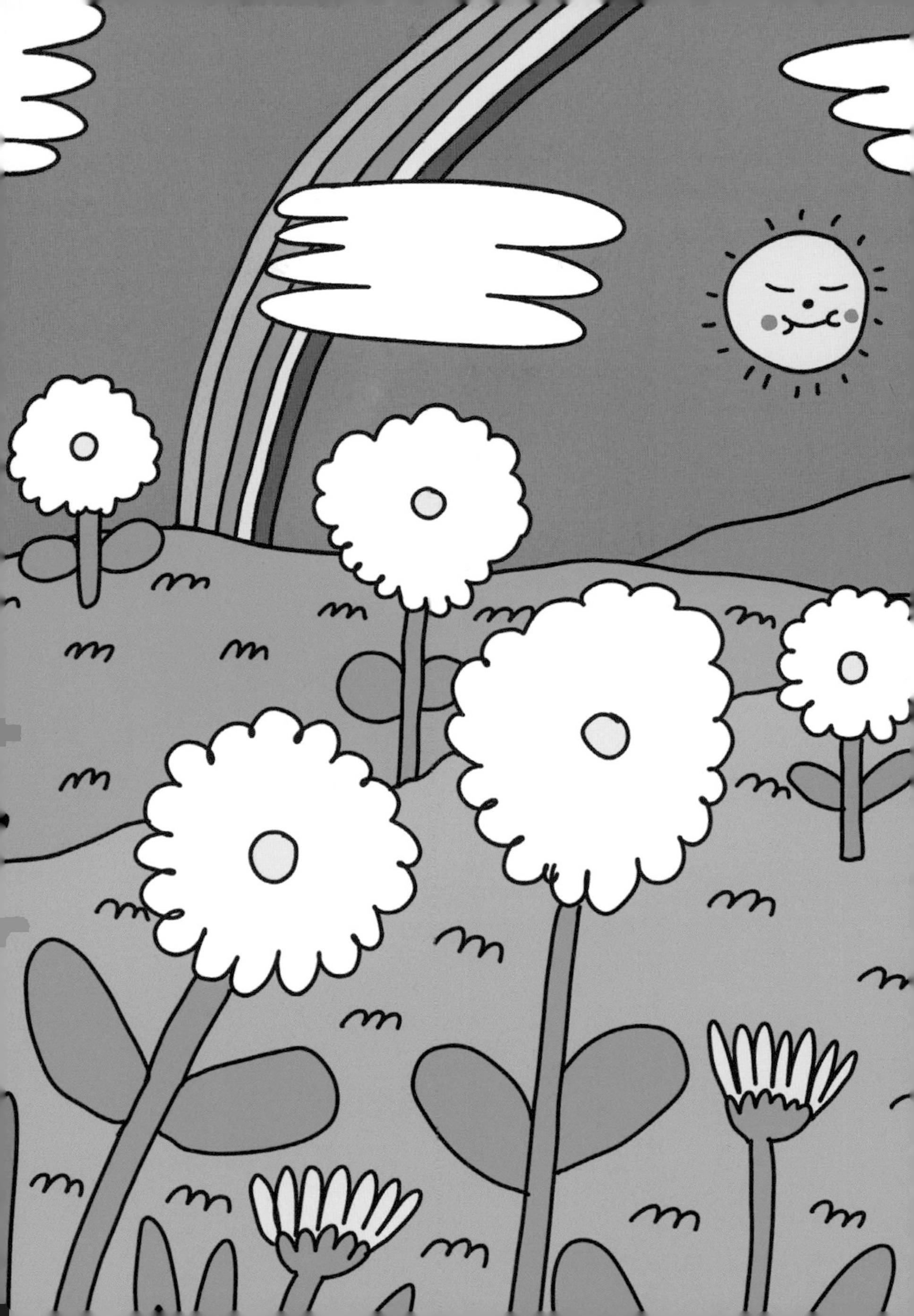

In this world, it can be easy
to lose sight of who you are.
It can be easy to begin to
resent aspects of yourself
that aren't 'perfect'.

What really is 'perfect' but
a tool to hold us back?

Who you are is whole.
So get out of your own way.
You deserve to love who you
are, with no second guesses.

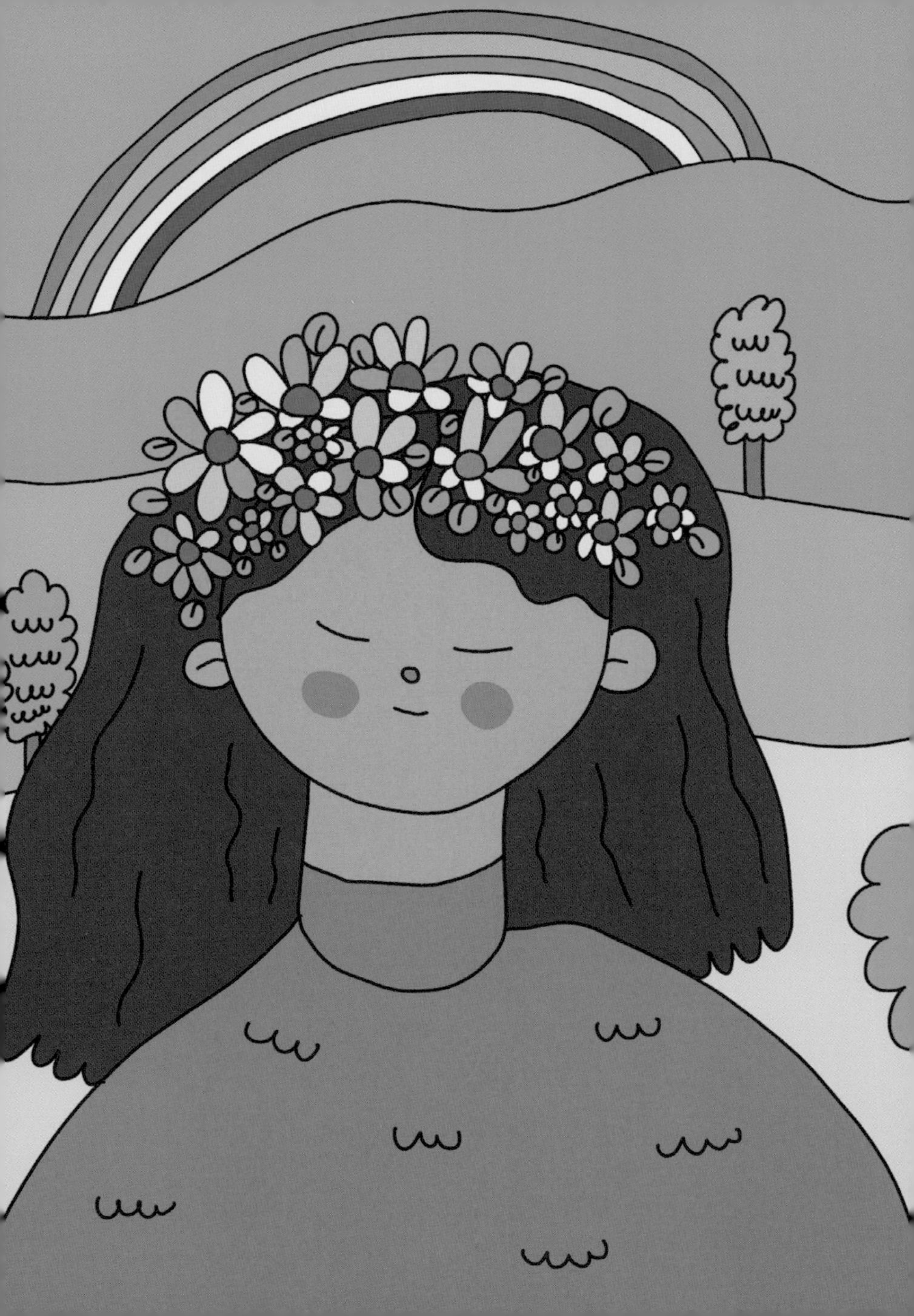

IDENTITY

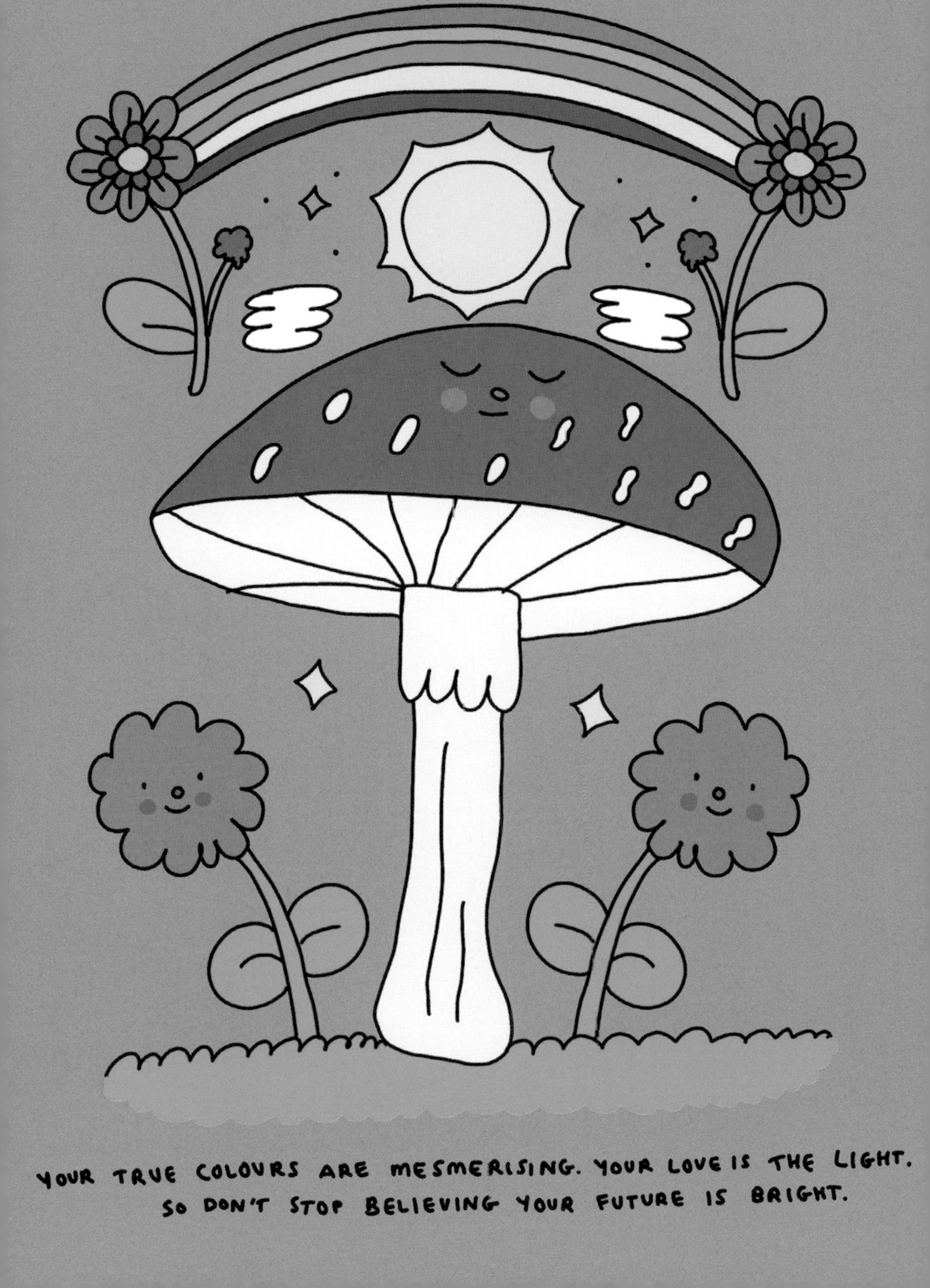

YOUR TRUE COLOURS ARE MESMERISING. YOUR LOVE IS THE LIGHT.
SO DON'T STOP BELIEVING YOUR FUTURE IS BRIGHT.

I hope you know that
when you stepped into
your authenticity, you
inspired someone else to
be authentic, too.

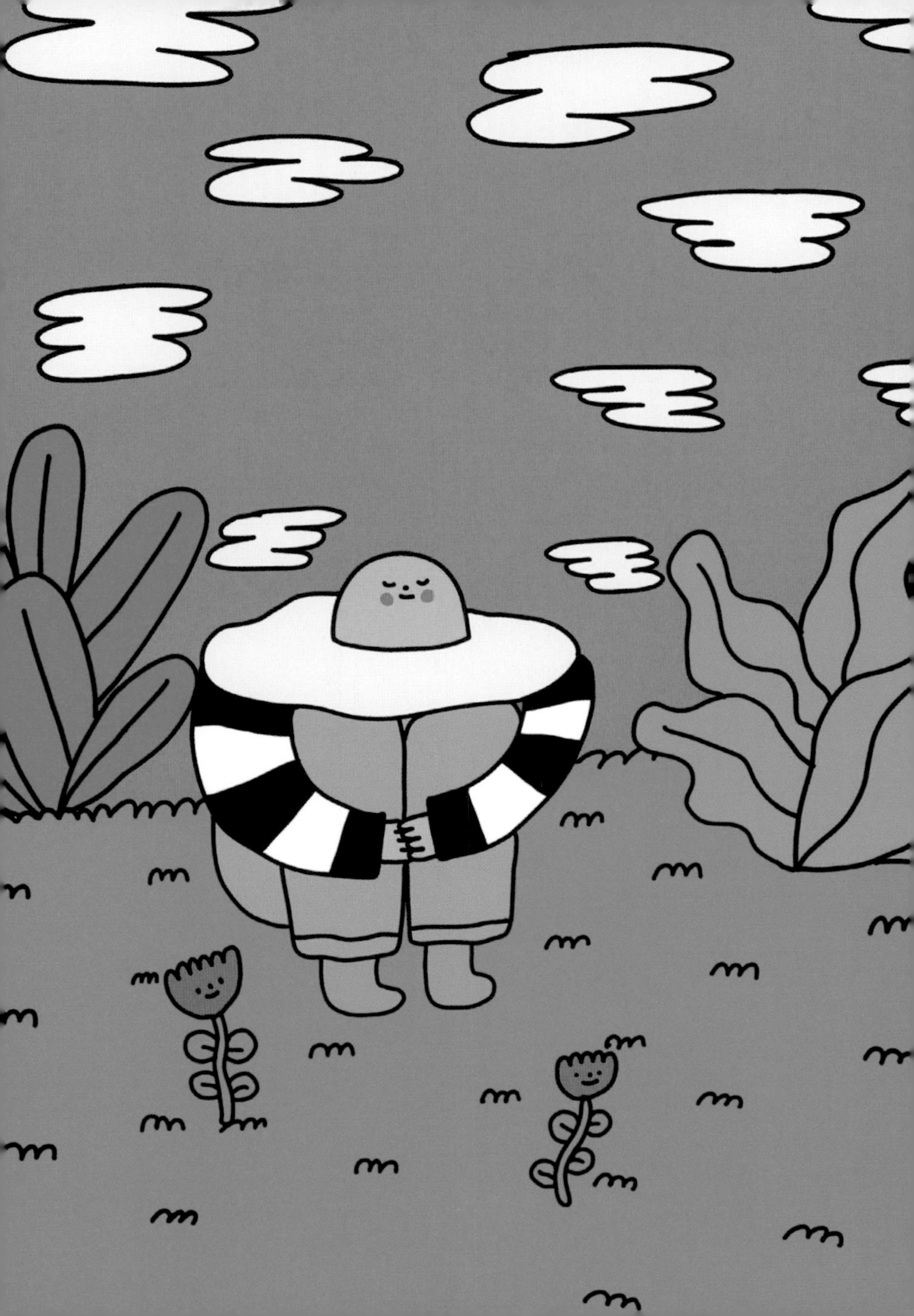

If there's one person we all
need, it's ourselves.

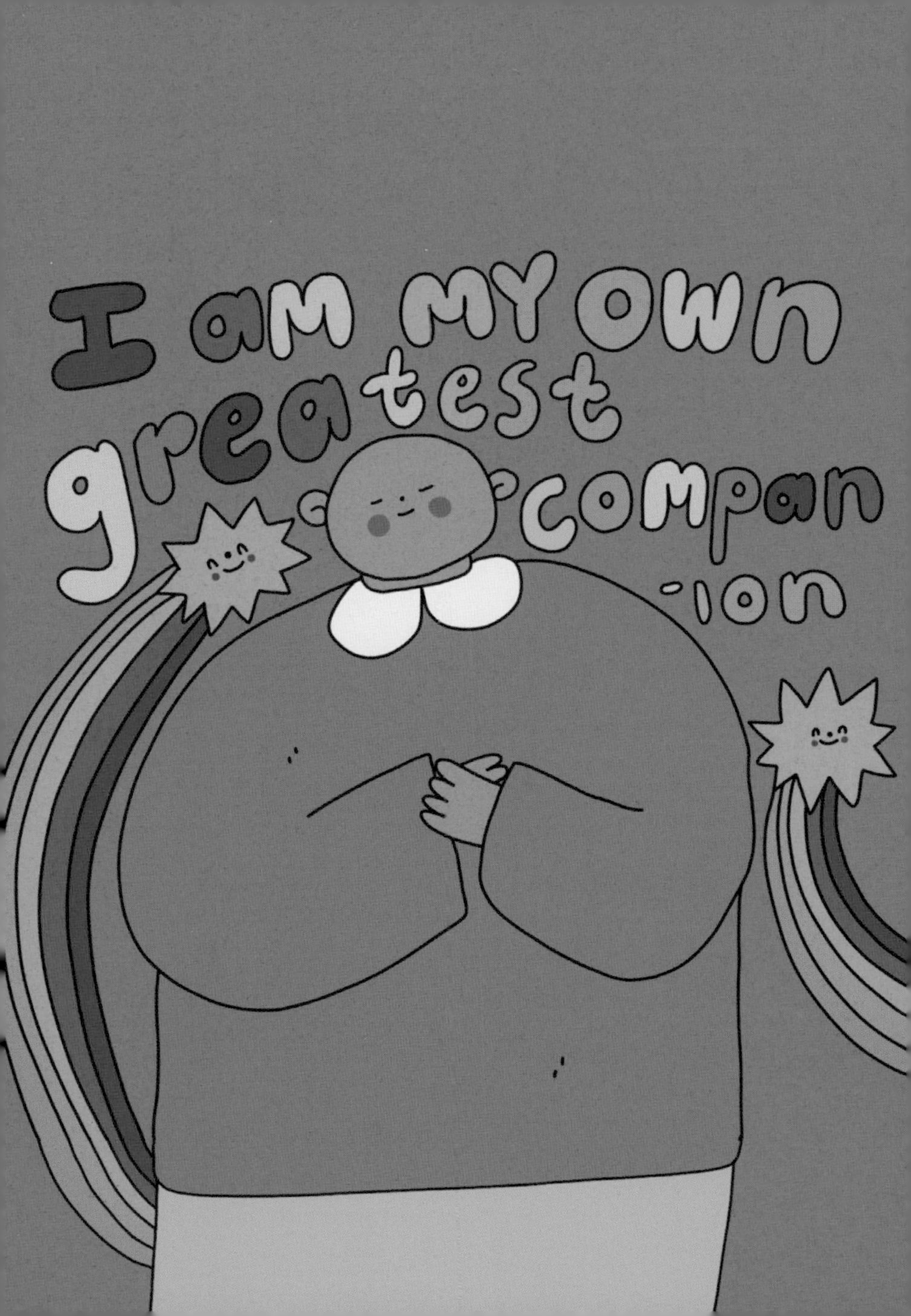
I am my own greatest compan-ion

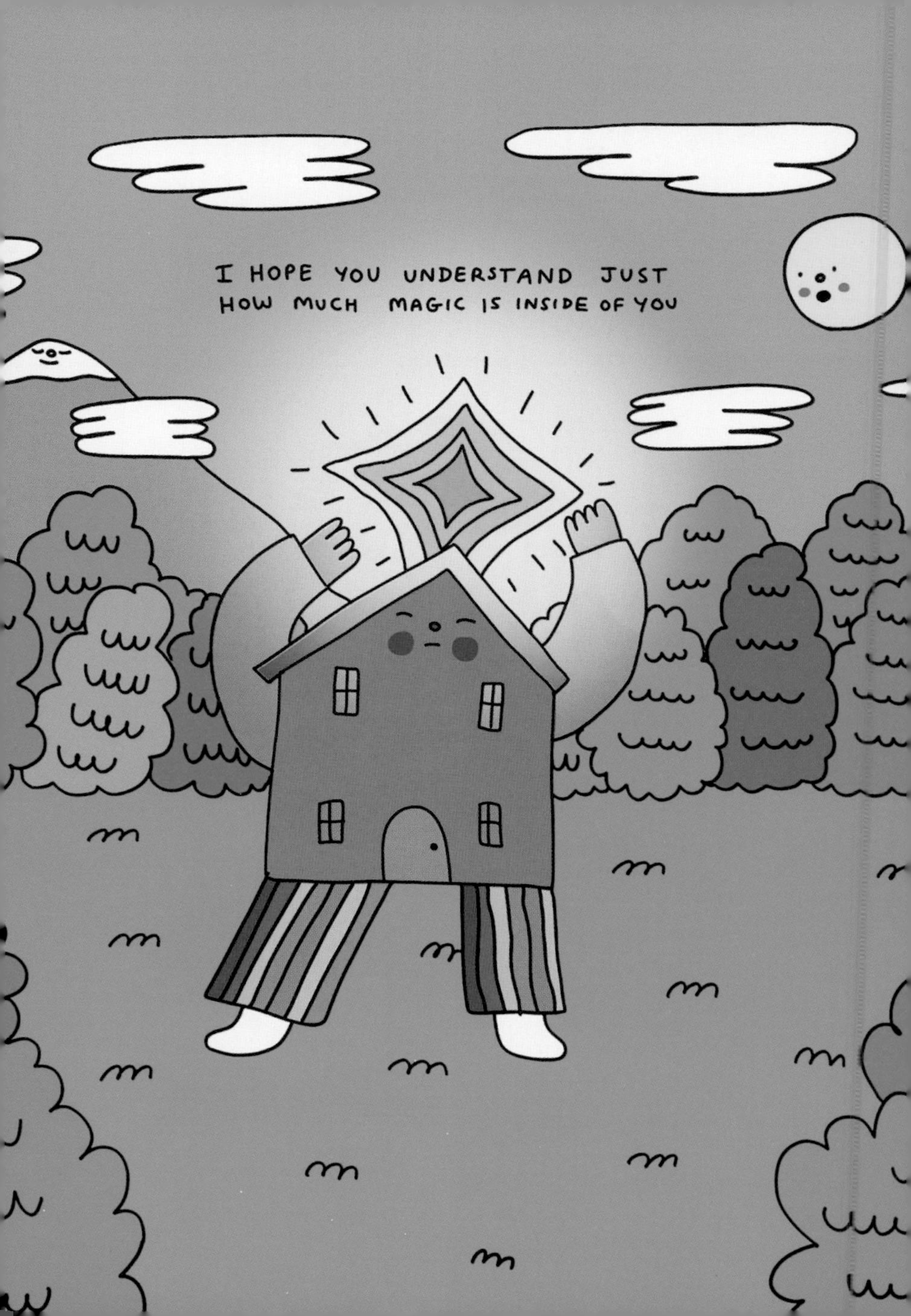
I HOPE YOU UNDERSTAND JUST
HOW MUCH MAGIC IS INSIDE OF YOU

You make this world better
just by existing.

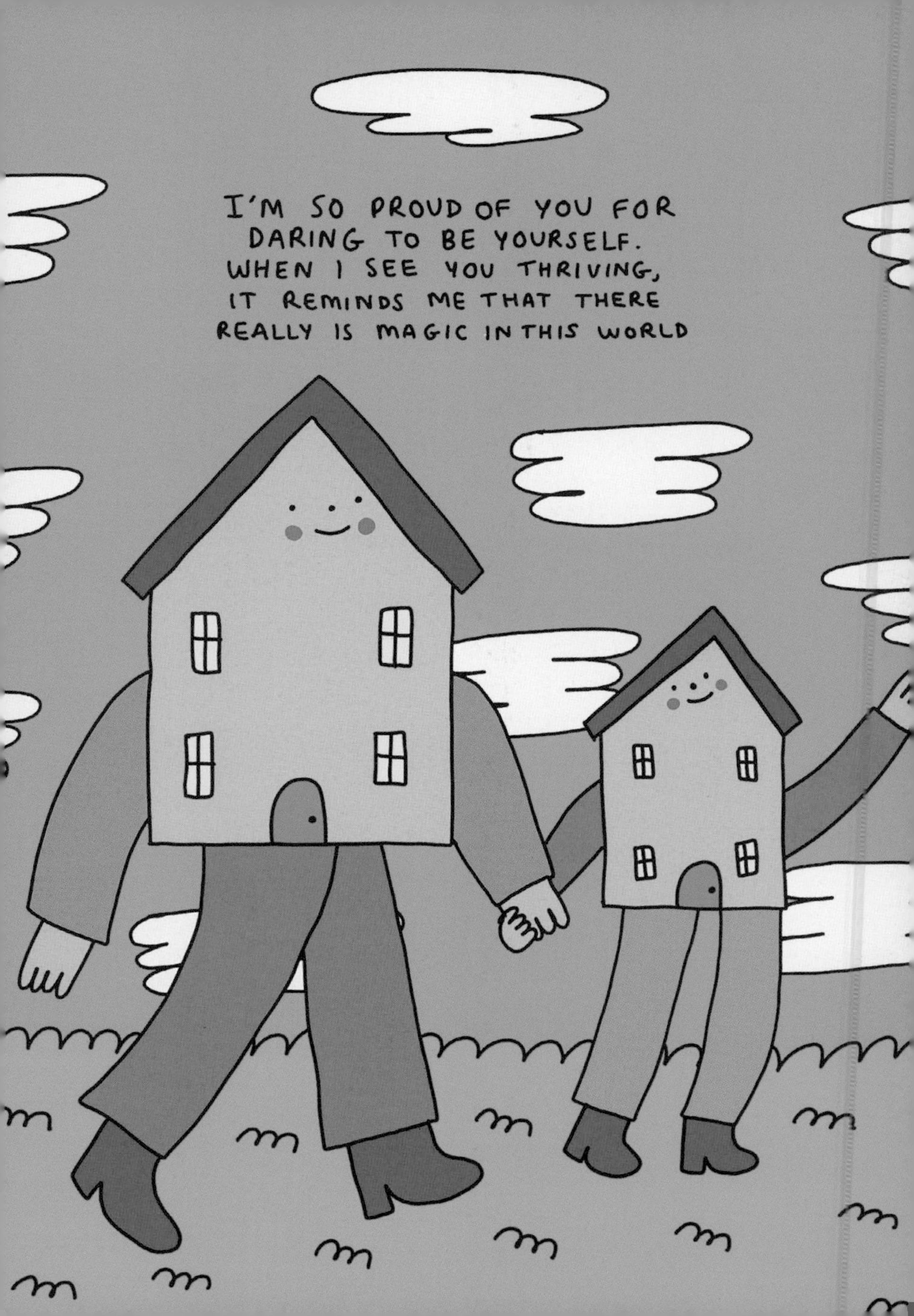
I'M SO PROUD OF YOU FOR
DARING TO BE YOURSELF.
WHEN I SEE YOU THRIVING,
IT REMINDS ME THAT THERE
REALLY IS MAGIC IN THIS WORLD

The younger you dreamed of becoming who you are today. Every move forward makes them proud. You lighten their world, so keep going.

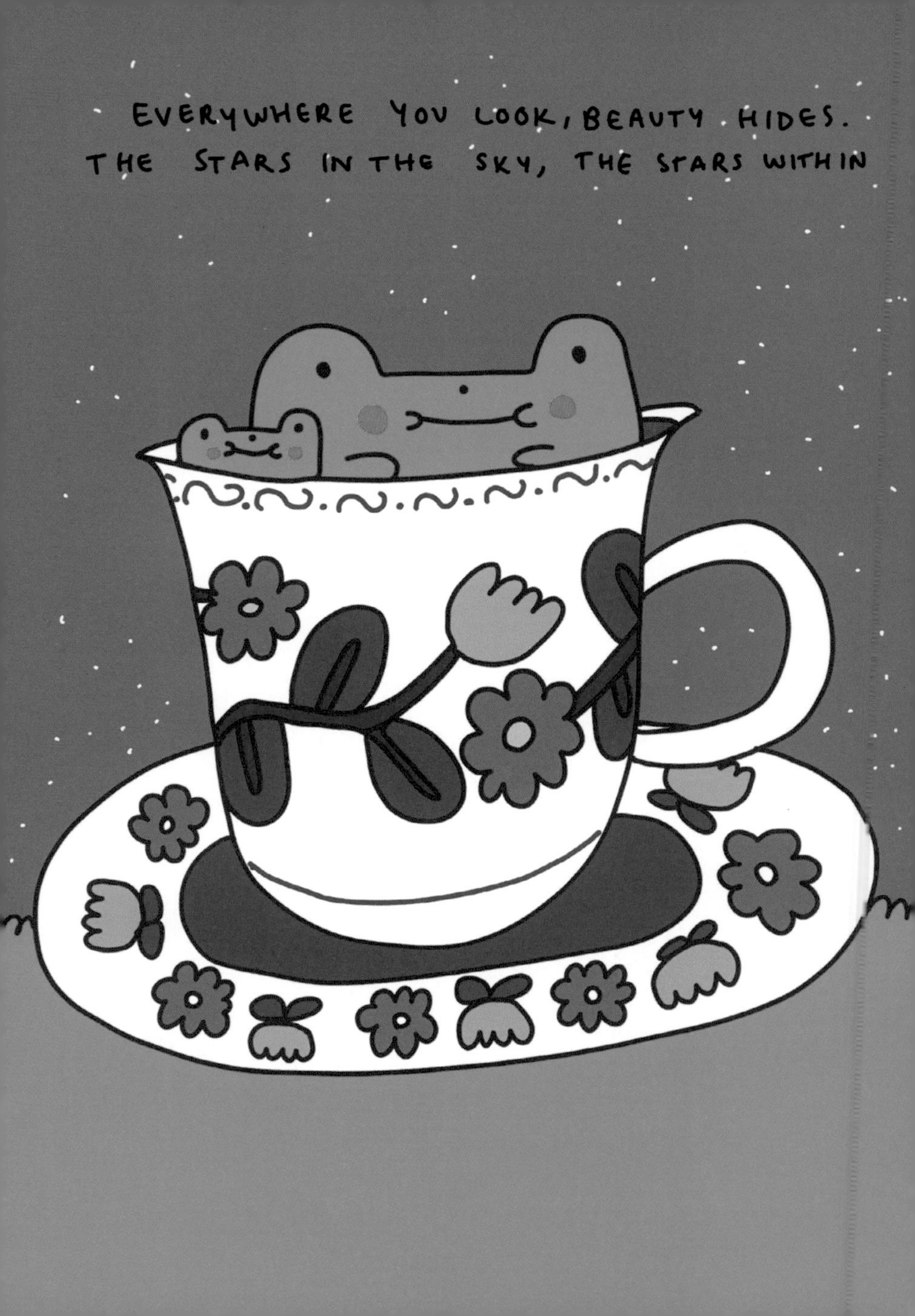
EVERYWHERE YOU LOOK, BEAUTY HIDES.
THE STARS IN THE SKY, THE STARS WITHIN

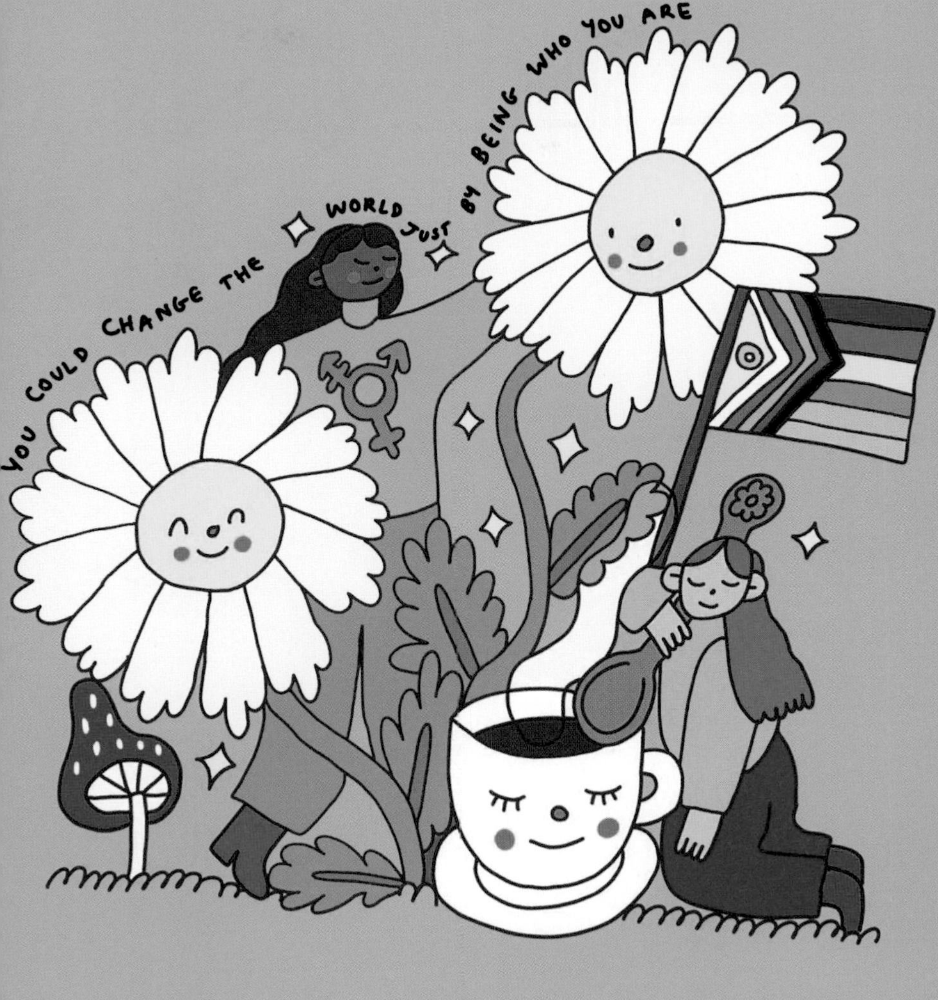
YOU COULD CHANGE THE WORLD JUST BY BEING WHO YOU ARE

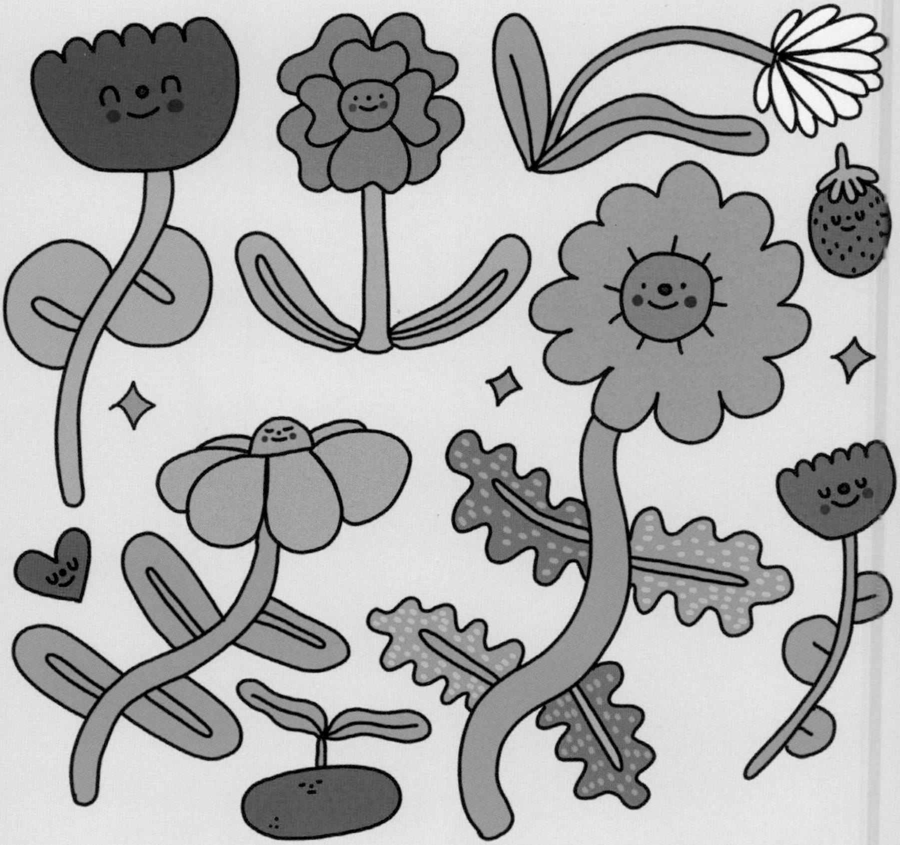

We aren't all supposed
to bloom in the same way.
That's the beauty of life.

You are full of light. A being bursting with stardust. A tree reaching through the canopy to reveal a sea of blue. Who you are is more than an Earth or sun or moon.

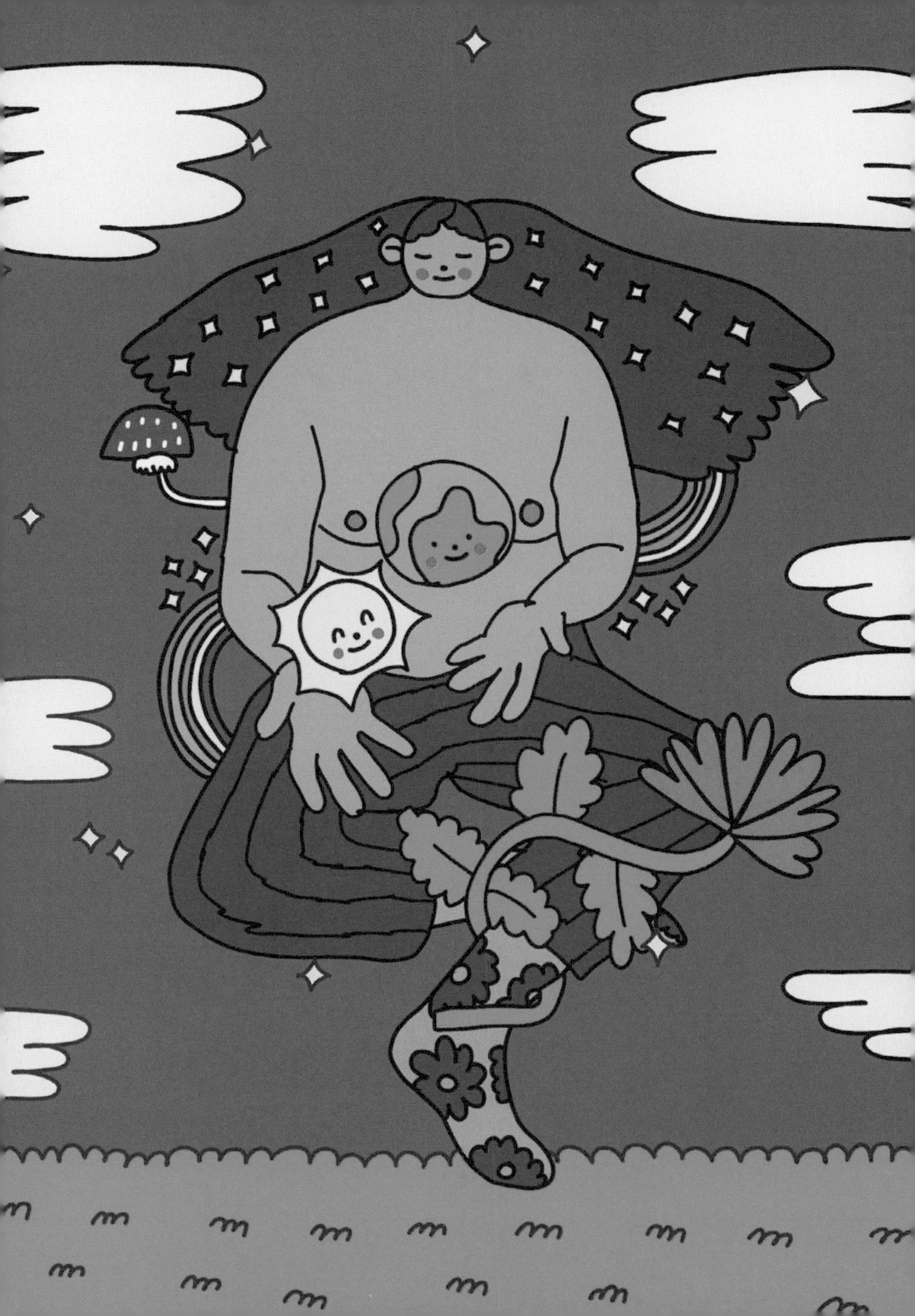

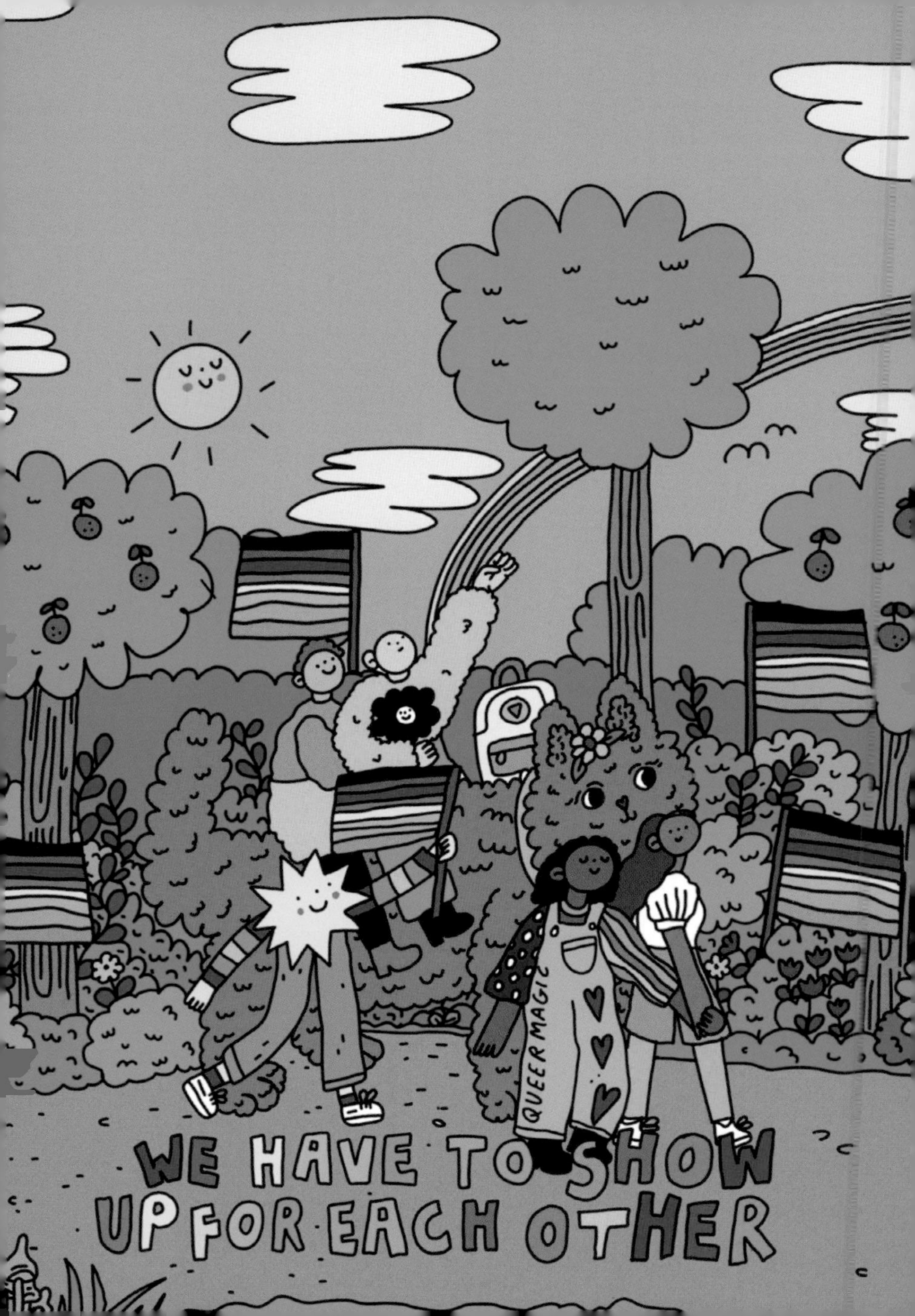
QUEER MAGIC
WE HAVE TO SHOW UP FOR EACH OTHER

Keep moving a foot at a time,
keep moving.

Keep moving outside the lines,
keep moving.

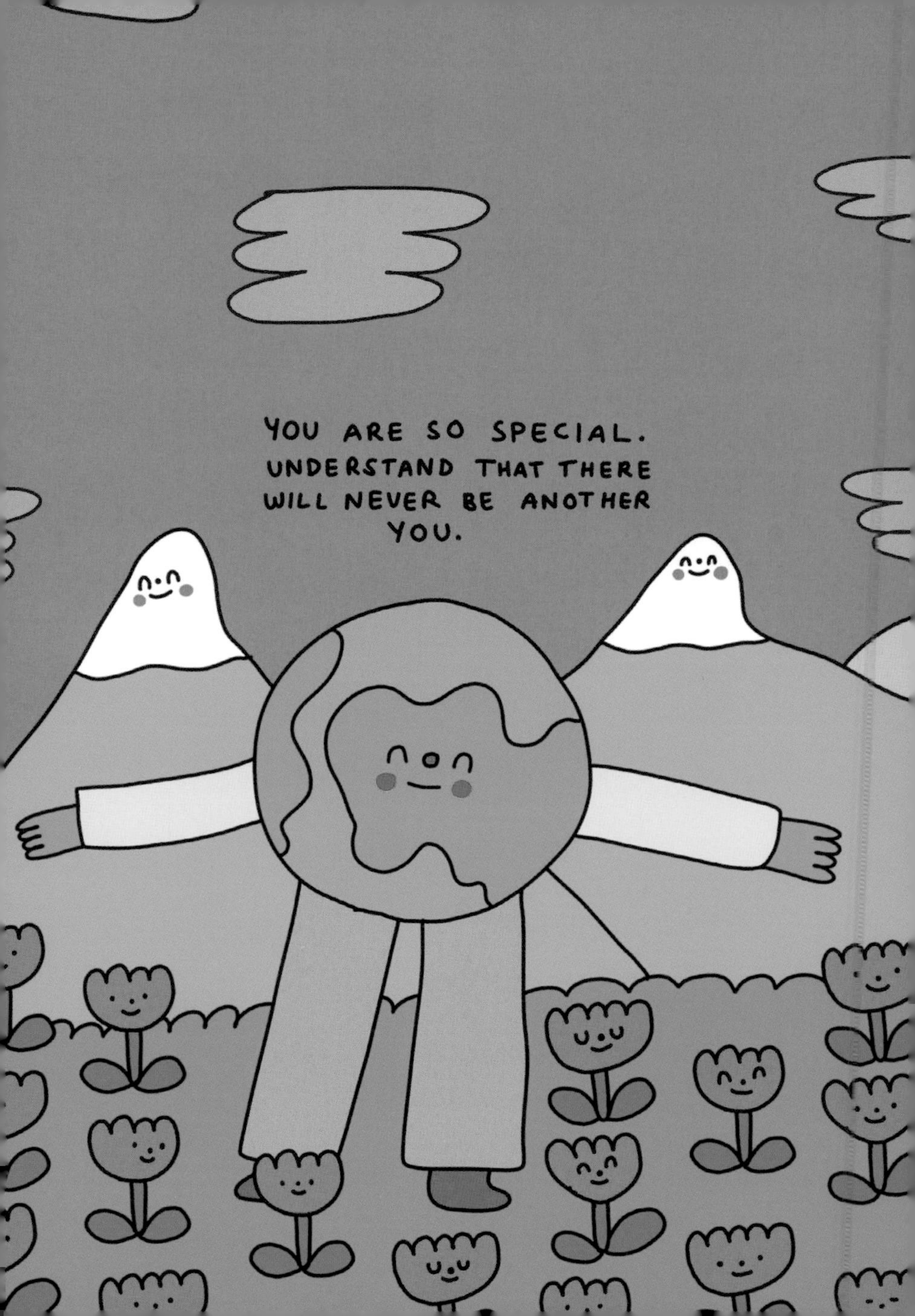
YOU ARE SO SPECIAL.
UNDERSTAND THAT THERE
WILL NEVER BE ANOTHER
YOU.

Your voice is needed,
despite what you've been told.

No matter what anyone says,
you are worthy, you are
loved, you are needed and
you are valued.

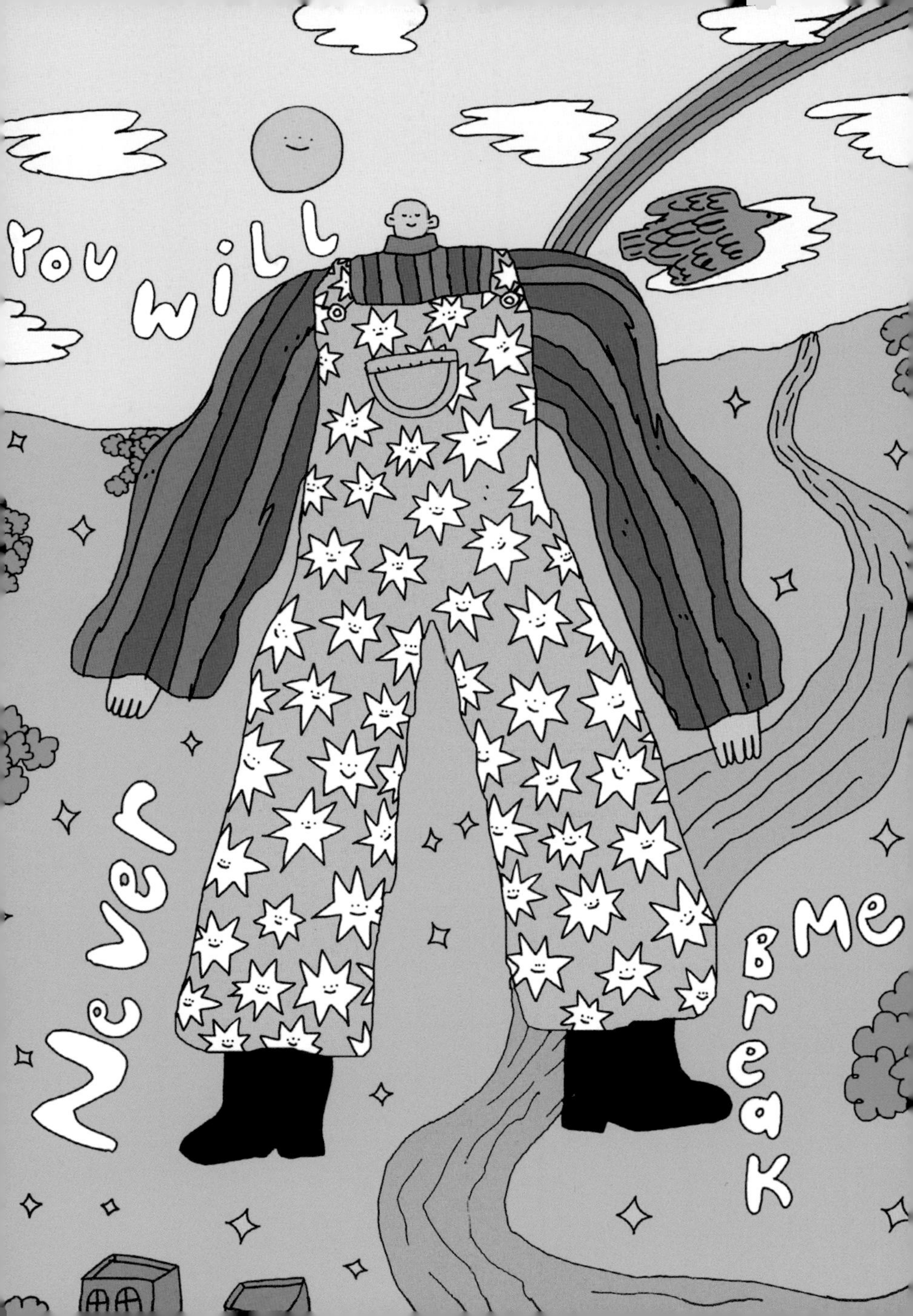
You will
Never
Break Me

GRIEF

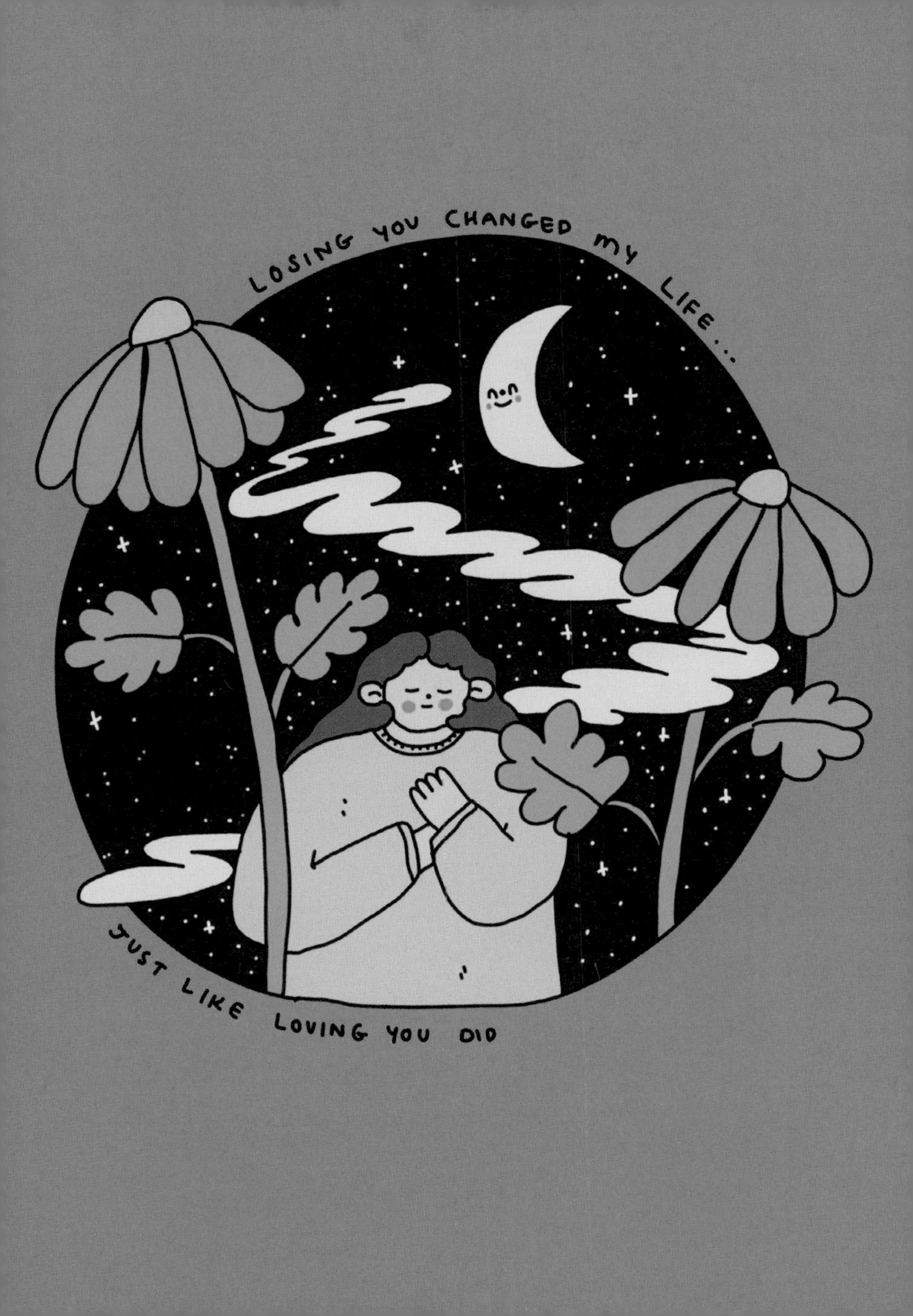
LOSING YOU CHANGED MY LIFE...
JUST LIKE LOVING YOU DID

JUST A LITTLE REMINDER THAT THE WORLD IS A CHALLENGING PLACE NOW. MAKE SPACE FOR REST AND THE THINGS THAT MAKE YOU HAPPY

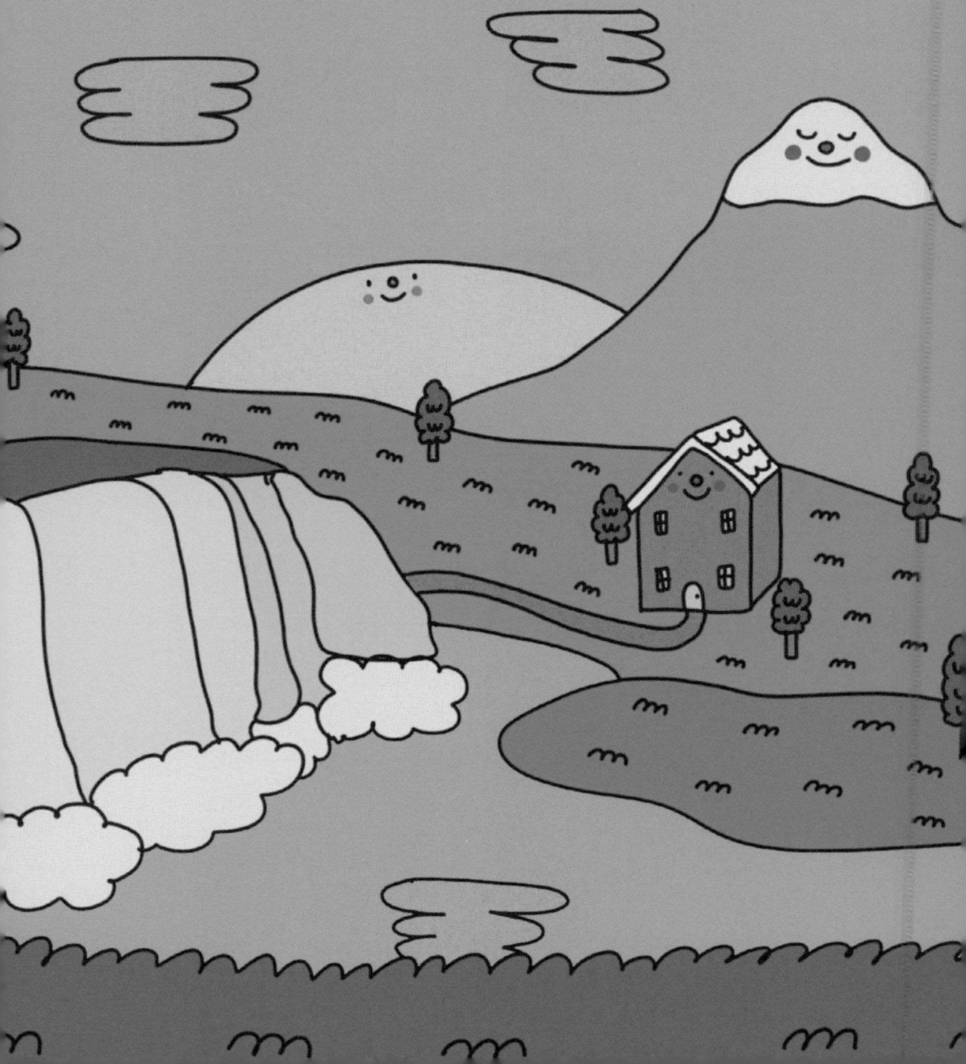

Sometimes the world can feel overwhelming. So remember to be oh-so gentle with yourself and get your rest. Resting isn't a reward or a gift, it's a necessity.

Take it easy, you are not a robot. You were meant to feel the softness of rest and the gentle calm. So don't forget to give yourself the space and love that you so generously give others.

I'm proud of you for
practising peace, even when
I feels like your world is
crumbling.

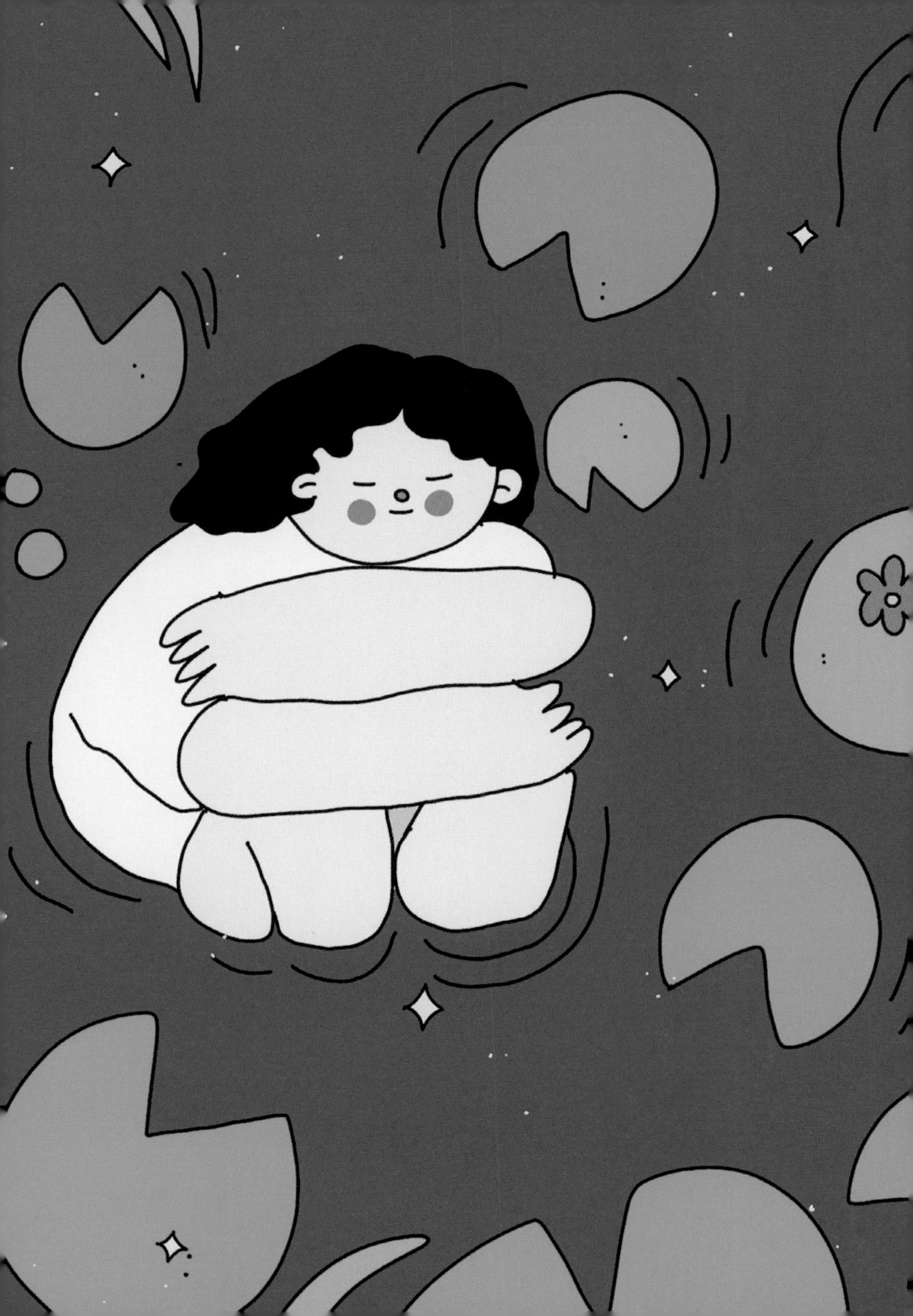

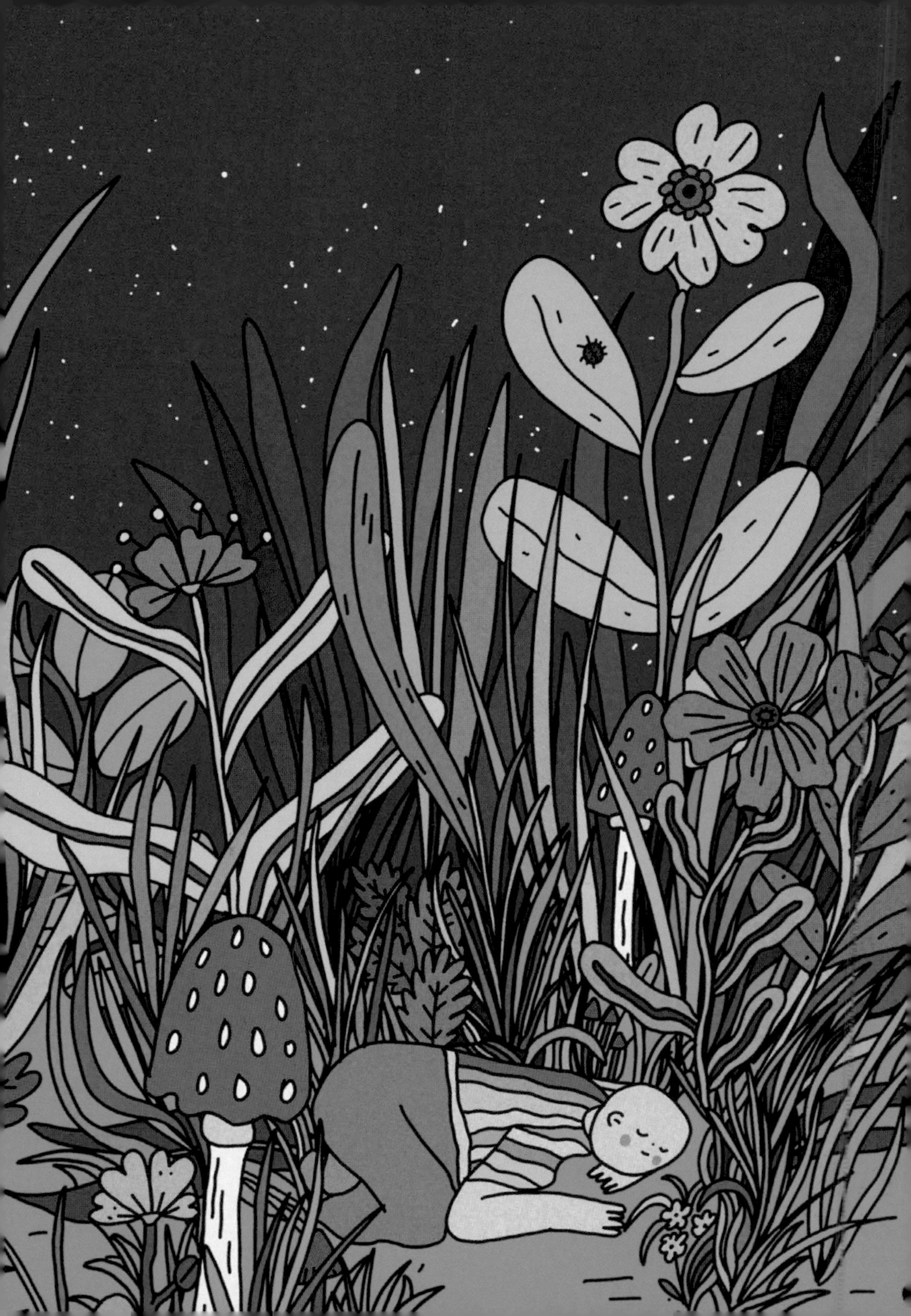

One day you will look back on these times with kinder eyes and realise that you did the best you could under difficult circumstances.

IT'S NEVER EASY, BUT IT'S TRUE THAT YOU DESERVE GROWTH AND RECOVERY

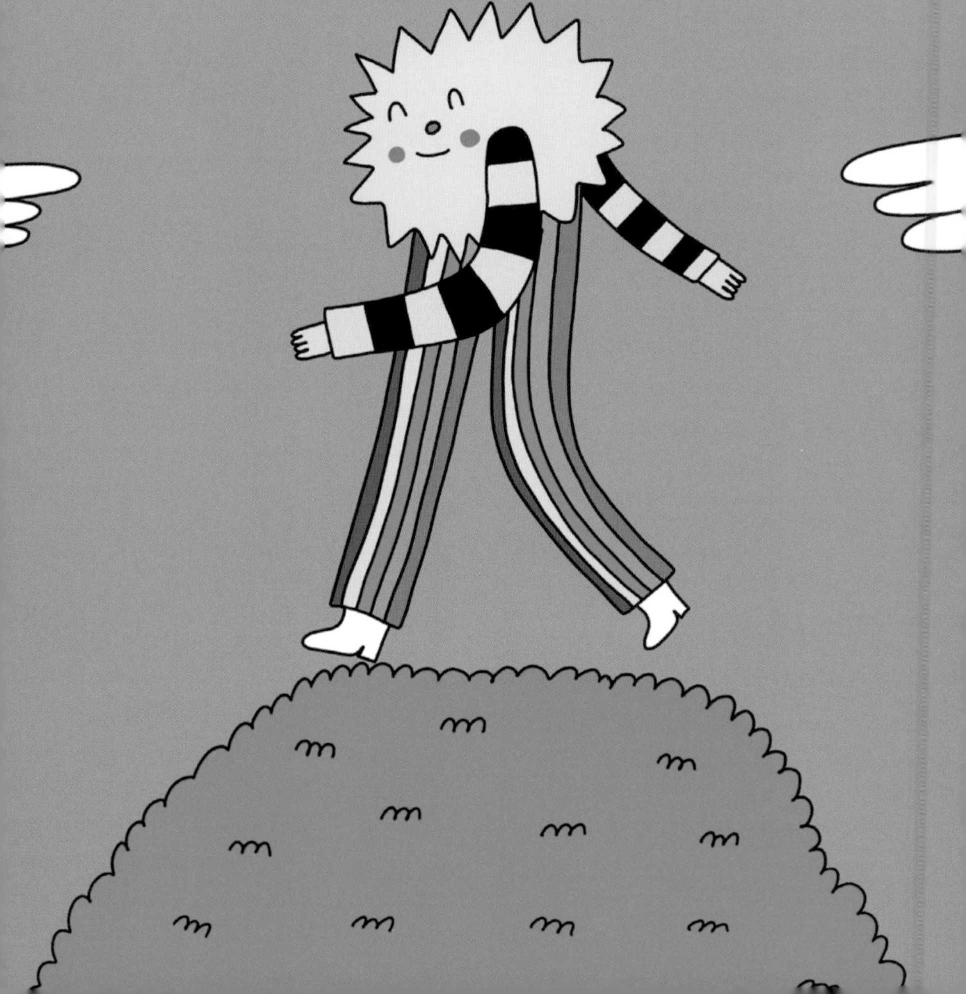

YOU ARE NOT A FAILURE BECAUSE HEALING IS TAKING LONGER THAN EXPECTED. YOU'RE ON YOUR OWN TIMELINE

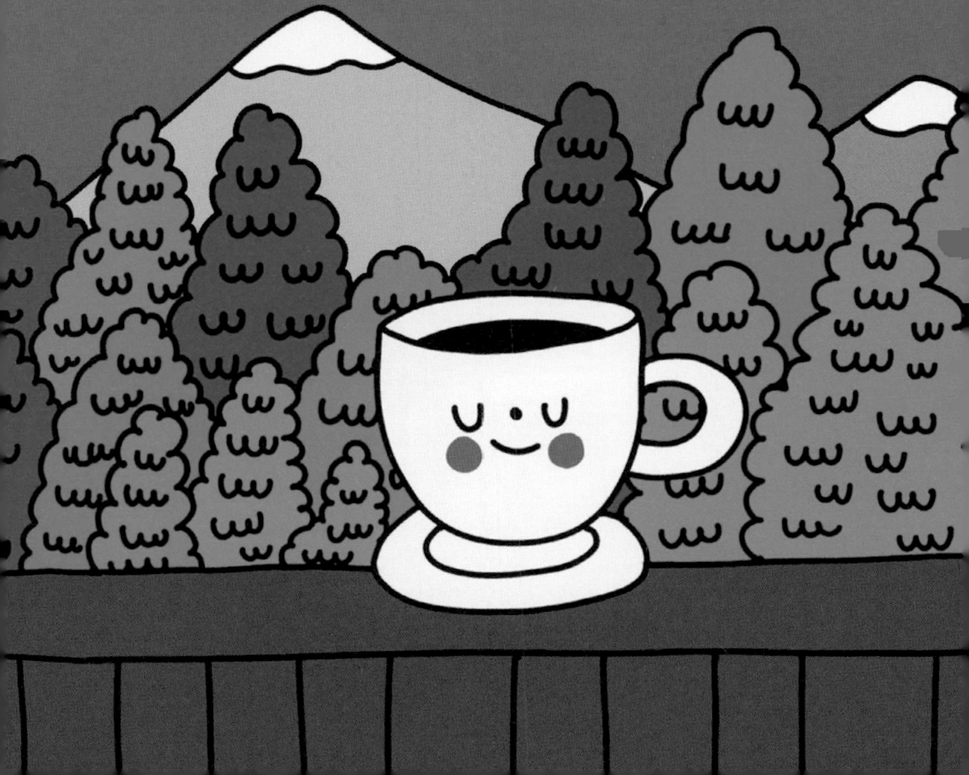

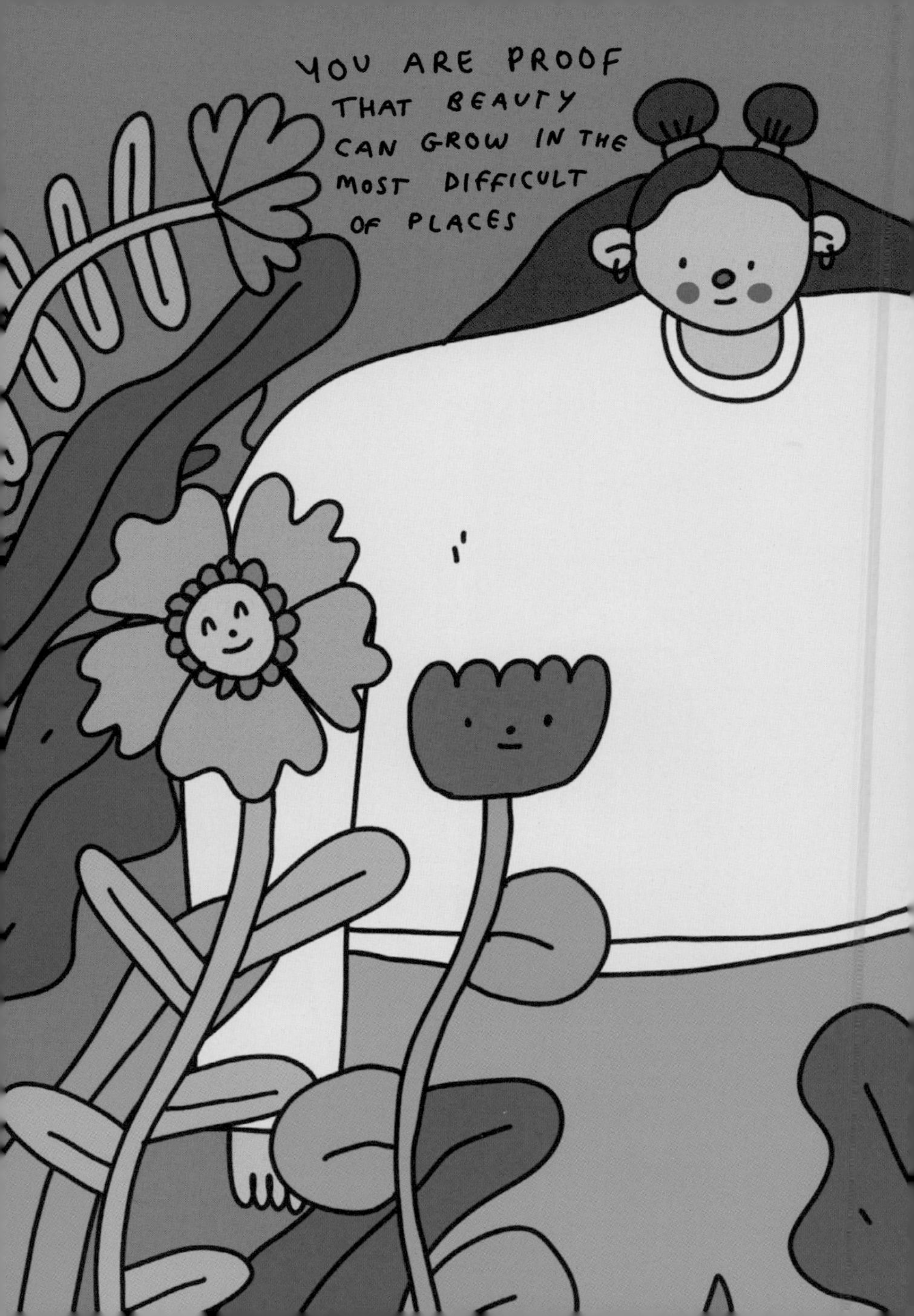
YOU ARE PROOF
THAT BEAUTY
CAN GROW IN THE
MOST DIFFICULT
OF PLACES

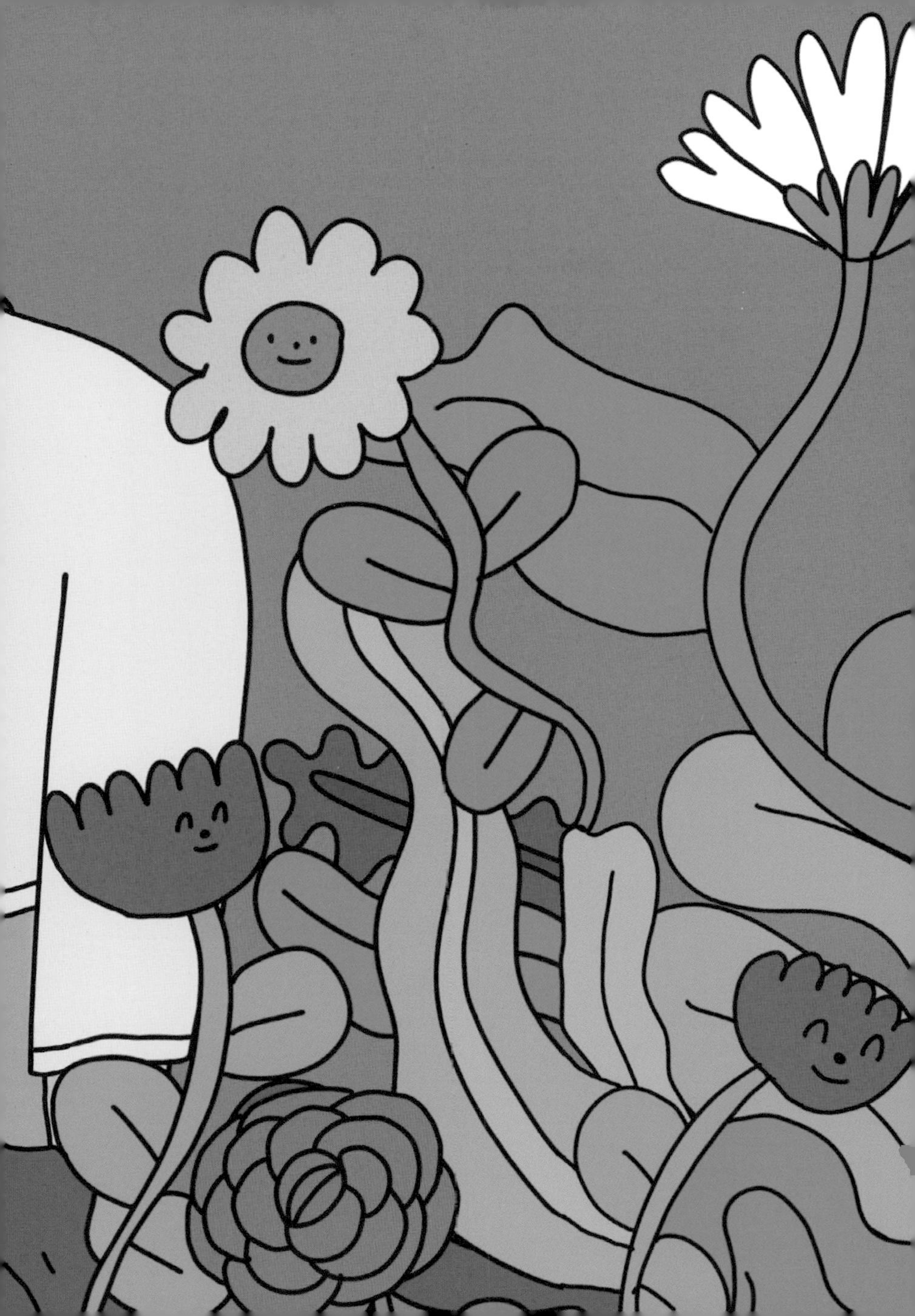

I'm so proud of you for
making it through the day.

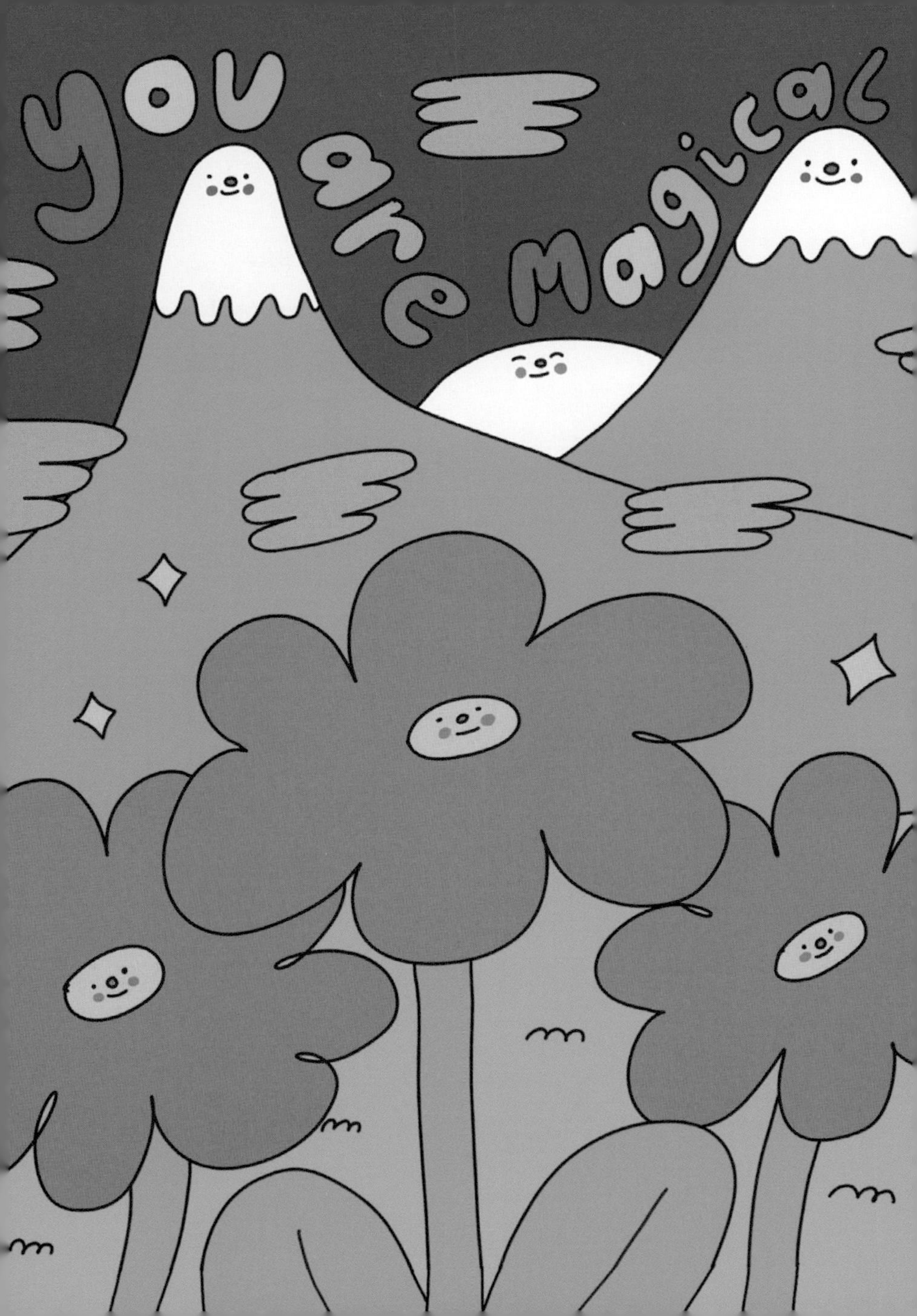
you are Magical

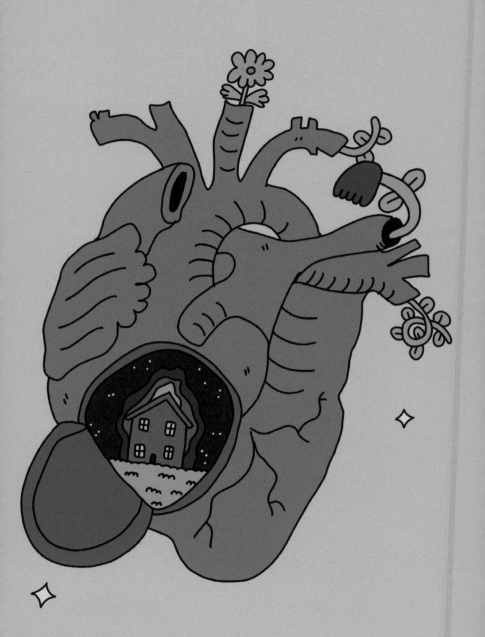

Some days there is no
reason for tears – let them
fall anyway.

May they water your flowers
that are yet to bloom.

You can't skip the hard parts
of healing – it's those parts
that help us to grow.

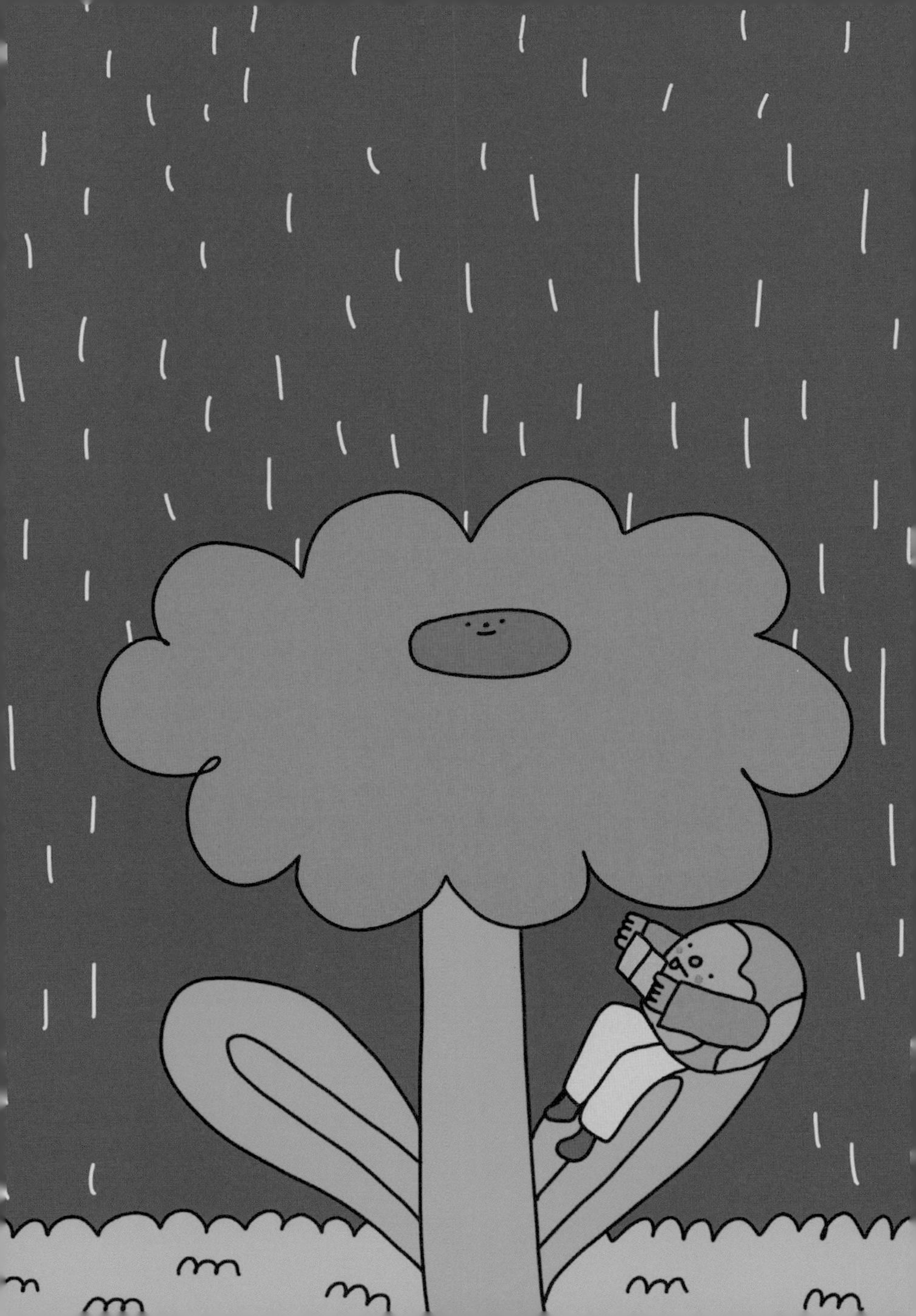

No one can tell you how to move on when someone leaves us. All you can do is keep moving forward with your heart in your hands.

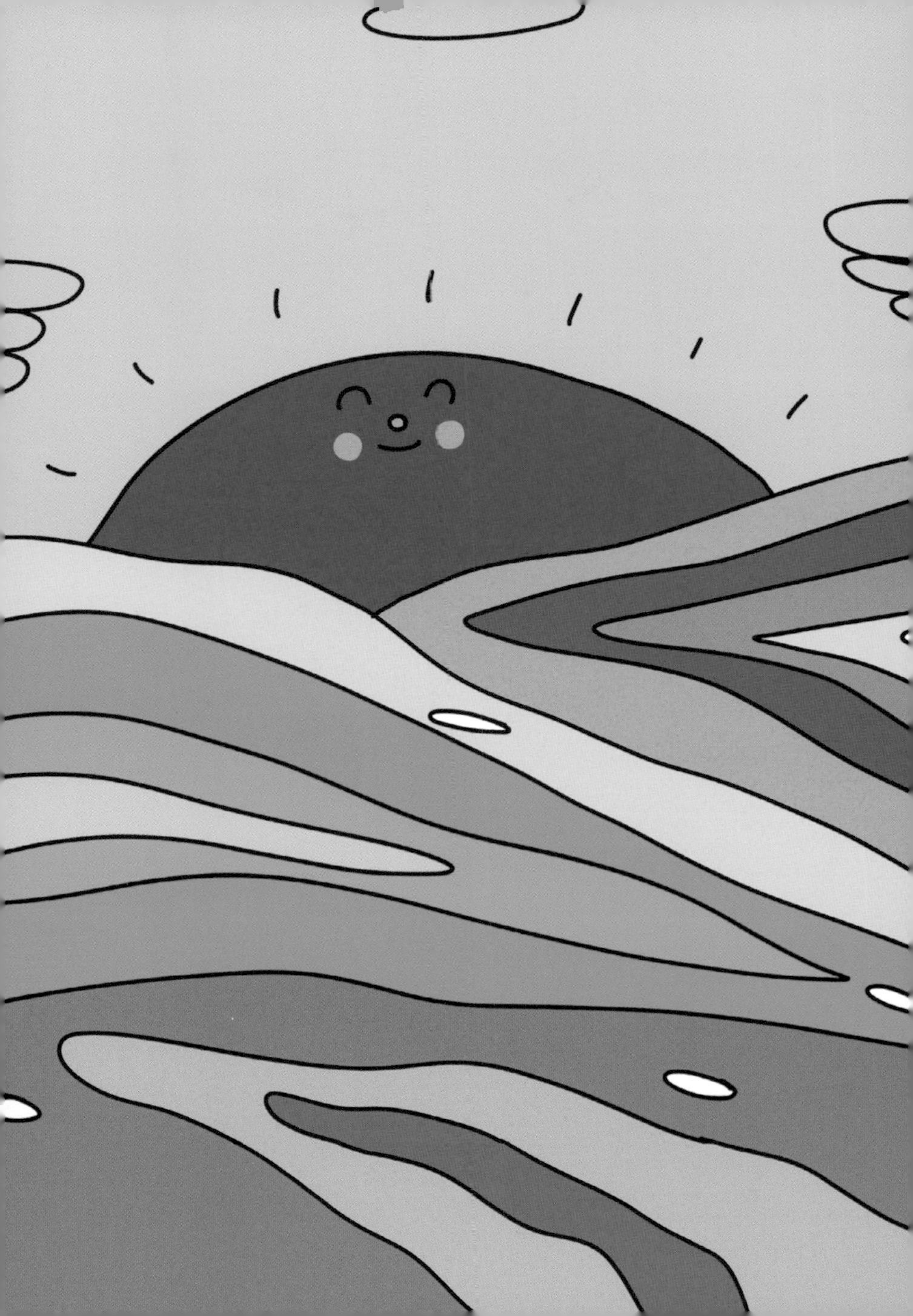

It will be OK in the end.
The sun is waiting to rise
just for you.

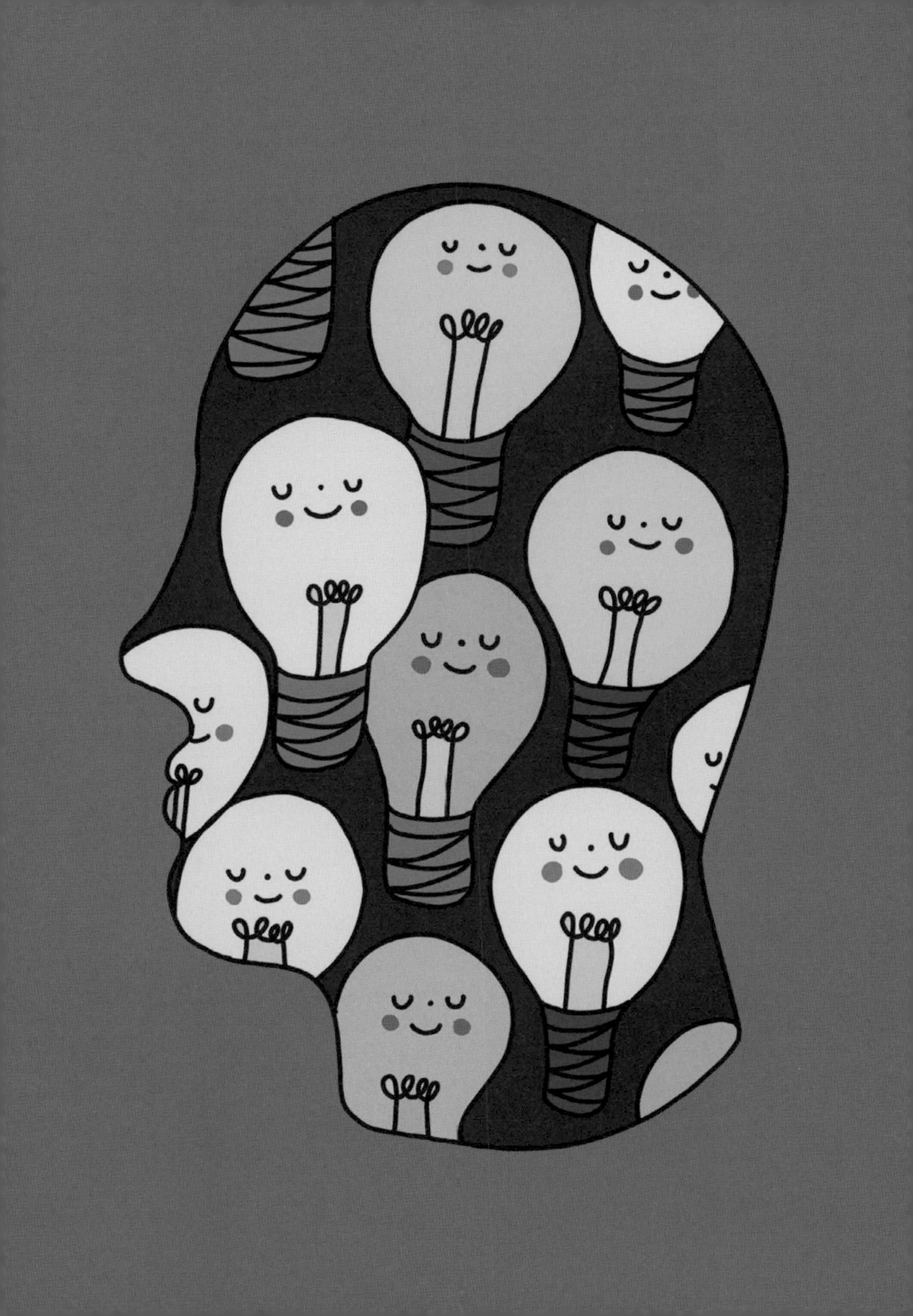

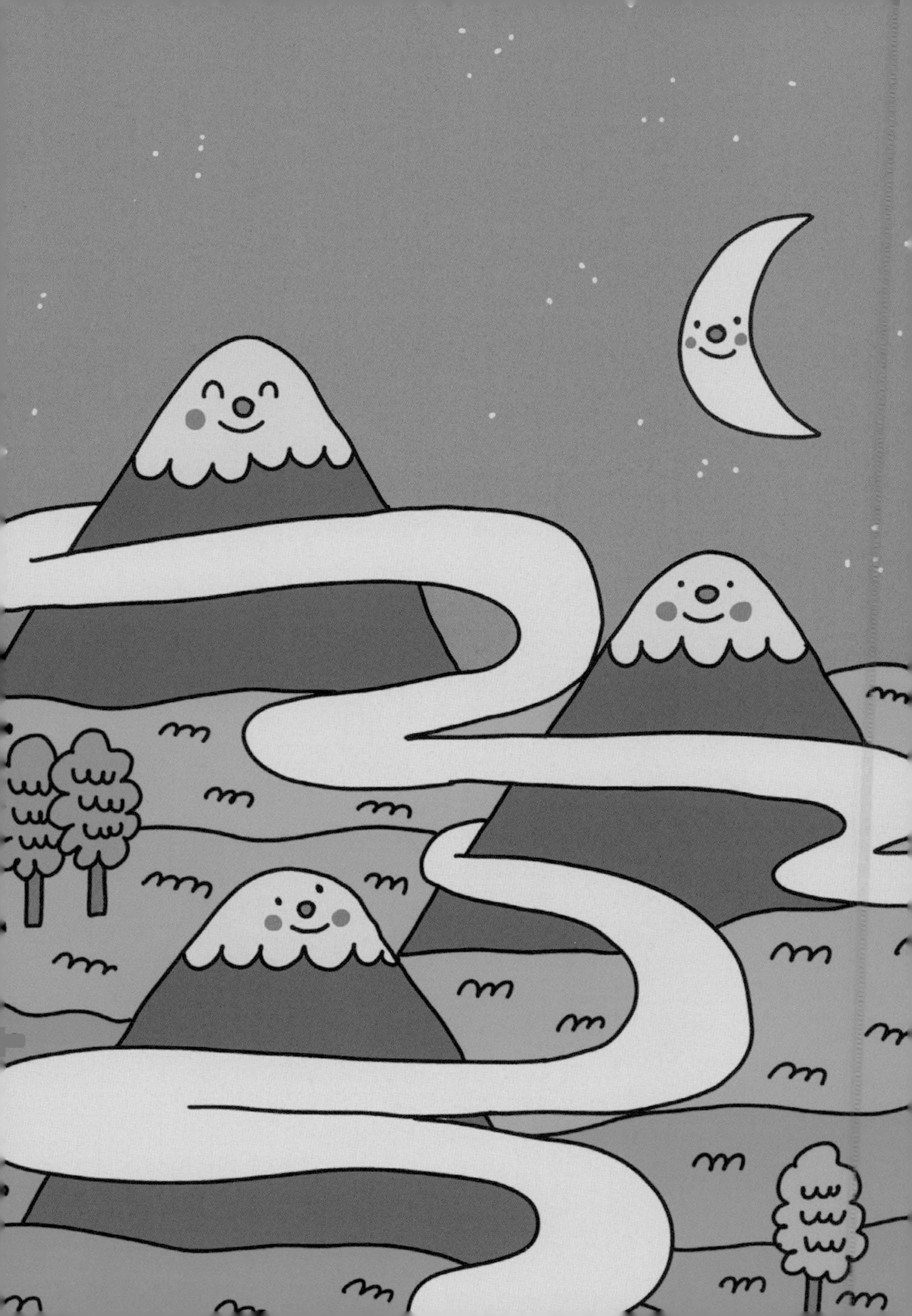

It's OK if your heart
aches for the past.

It's OK to miss someone so
deeply that you feel you
cannot rise up.

You will find the strength
to burst open like a bud
of a flower.

You will show us all what it
is like to grow and shine,
despite the darkness.

AFFIRM

THE BEST BITS ARE YET TO COME, SO STICK AROUND AND YOU'LL FIND OUT

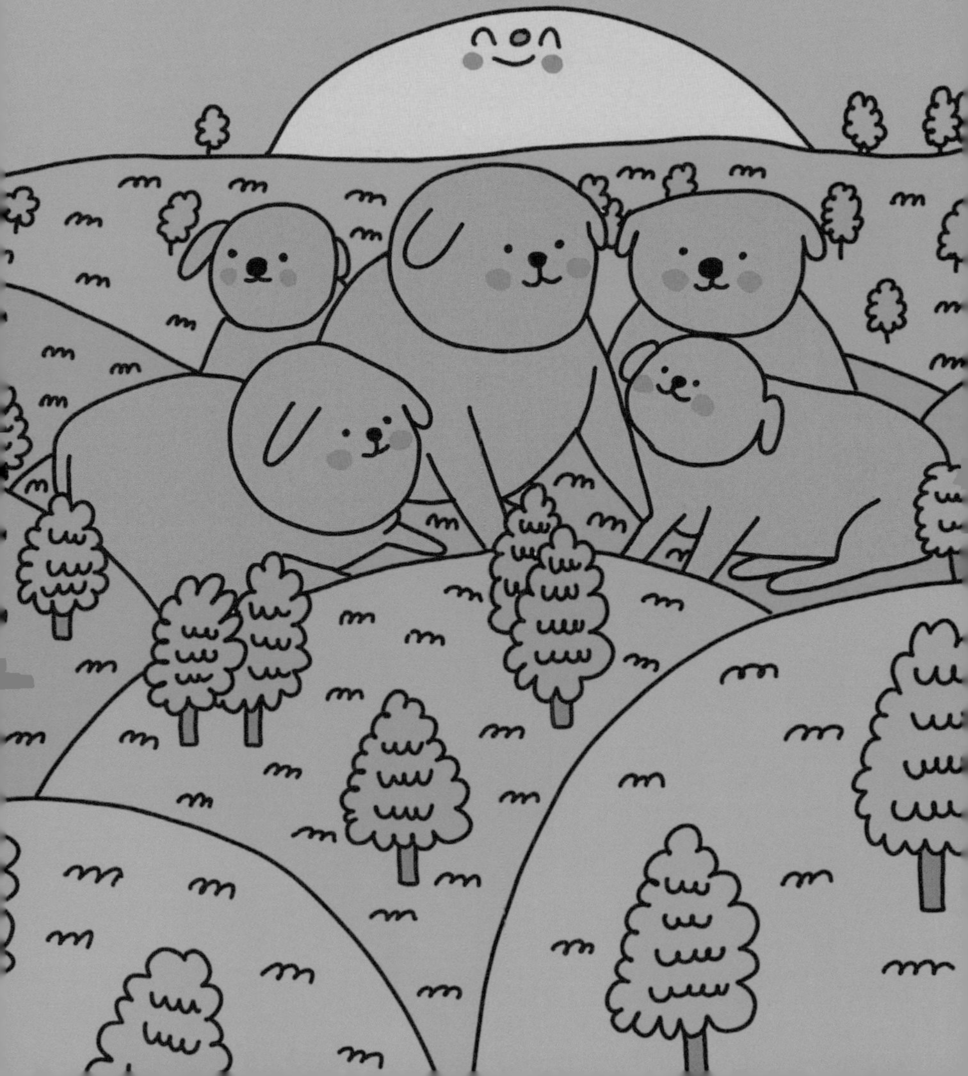

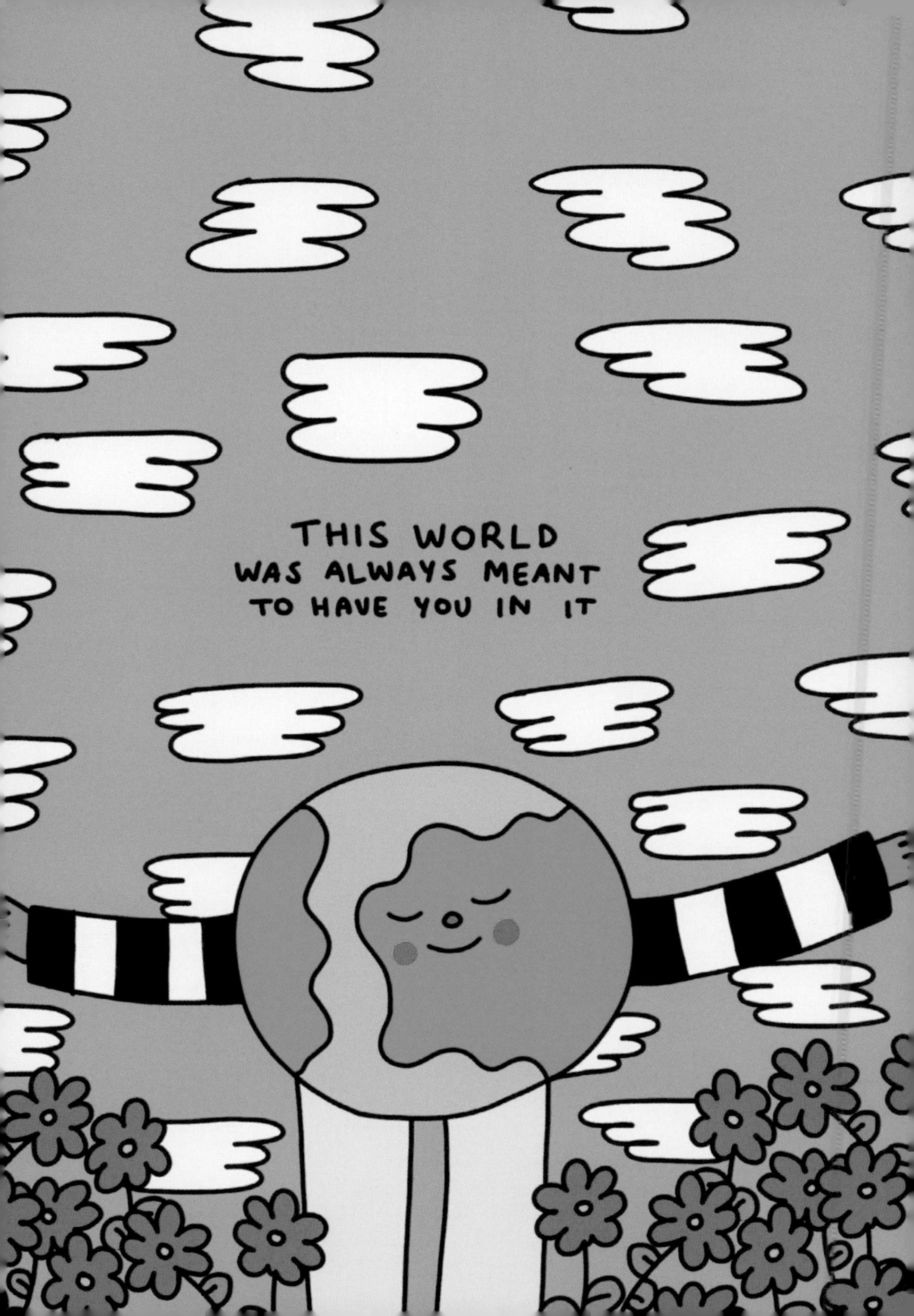
THIS WORLD
WAS ALWAYS MEANT
TO HAVE YOU IN IT

You made it.

You're here. Even after
everything you've
been through.

So just in case no one has said
this lately, I'm so proud of
you. I see you taking up space
for yourself. I see you. You are
doing so well under these
tough circumstances.

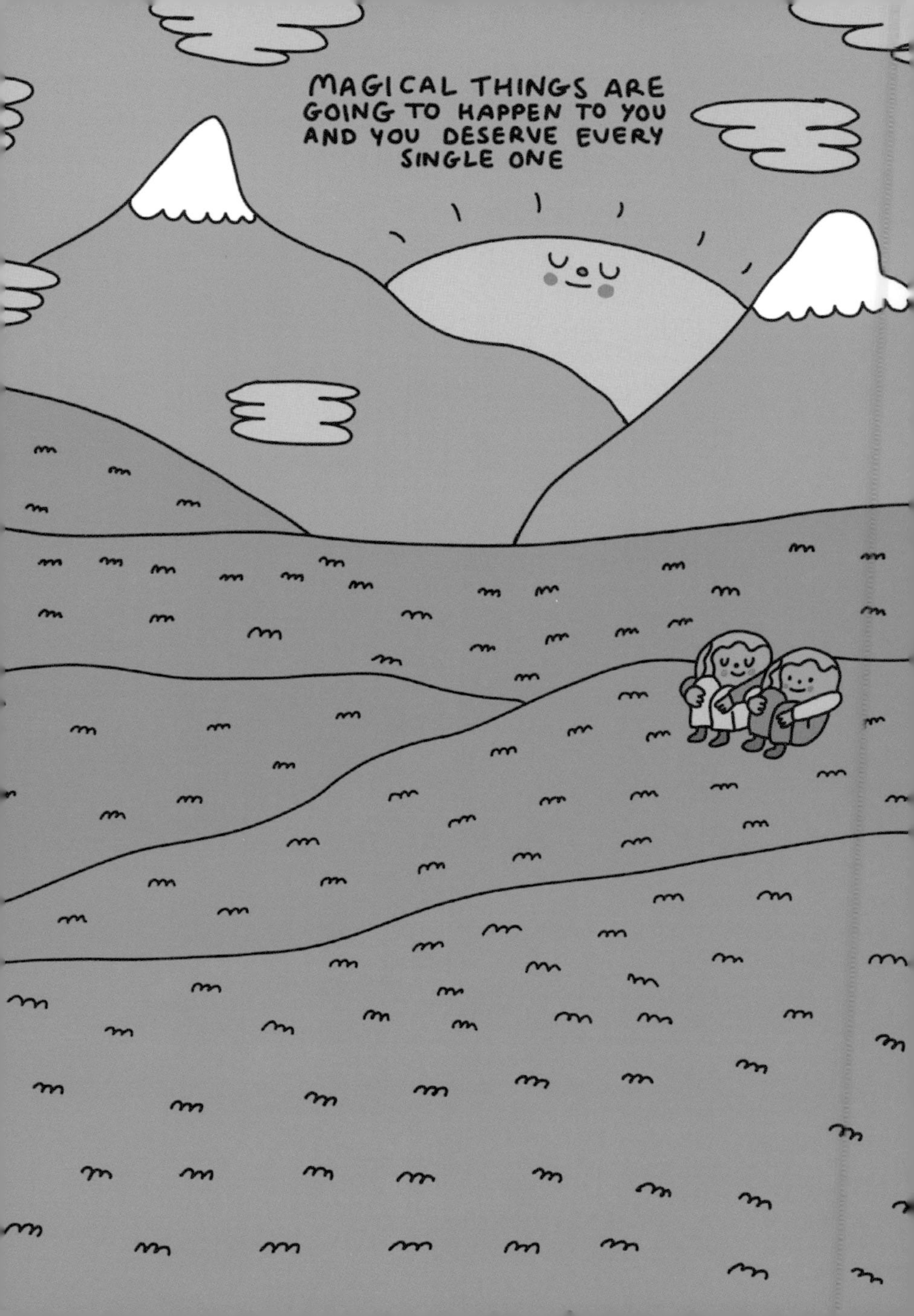
MAGICAL THINGS ARE GOING TO HAPPEN TO YOU AND YOU DESERVE EVERY SINGLE ONE

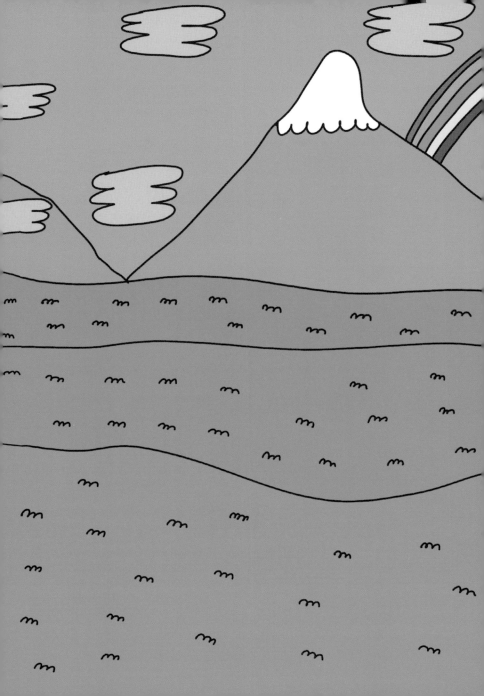

May the world fit to the
shape of your peace.
May your feet feel the grass
and turn to flowers.

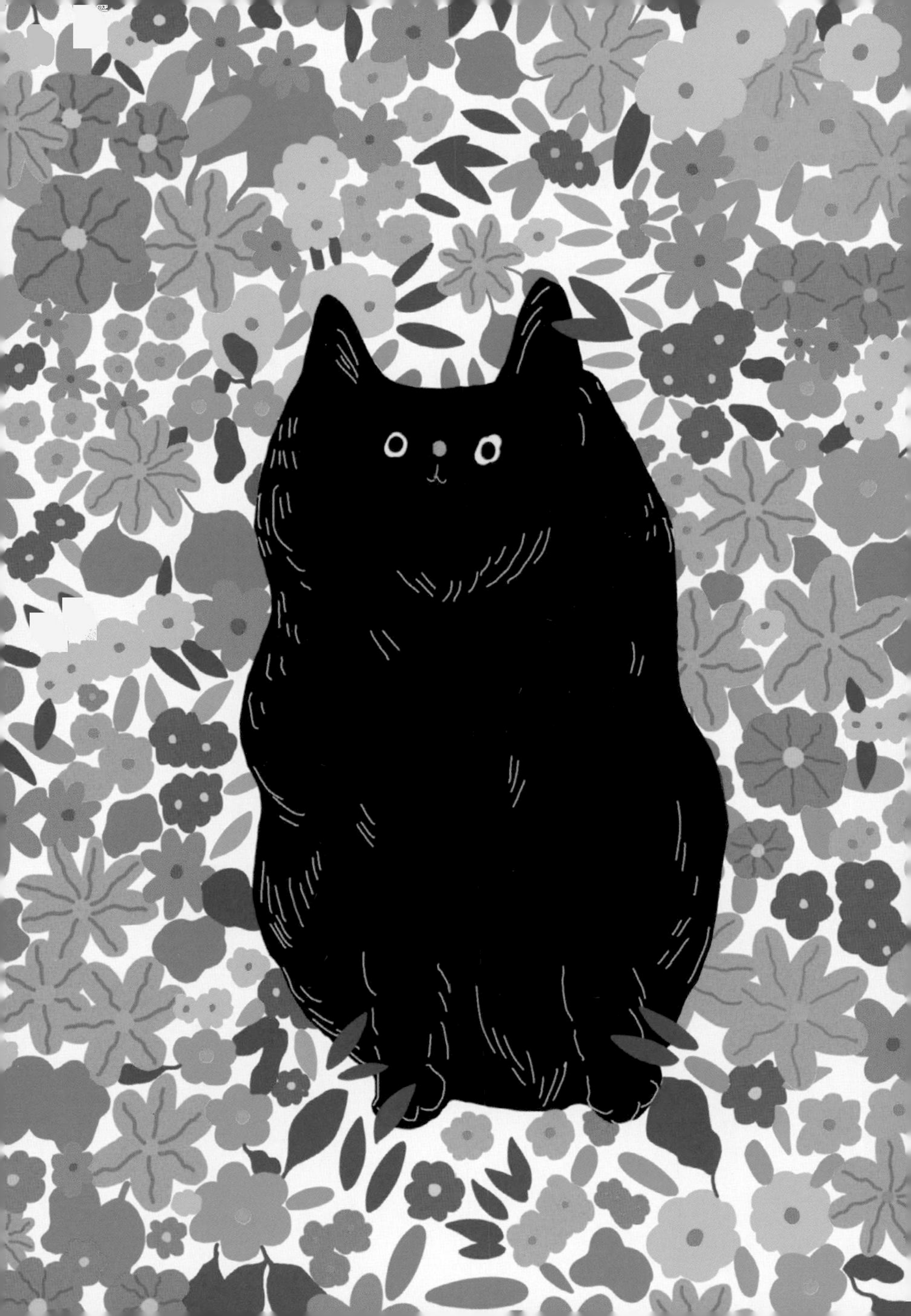

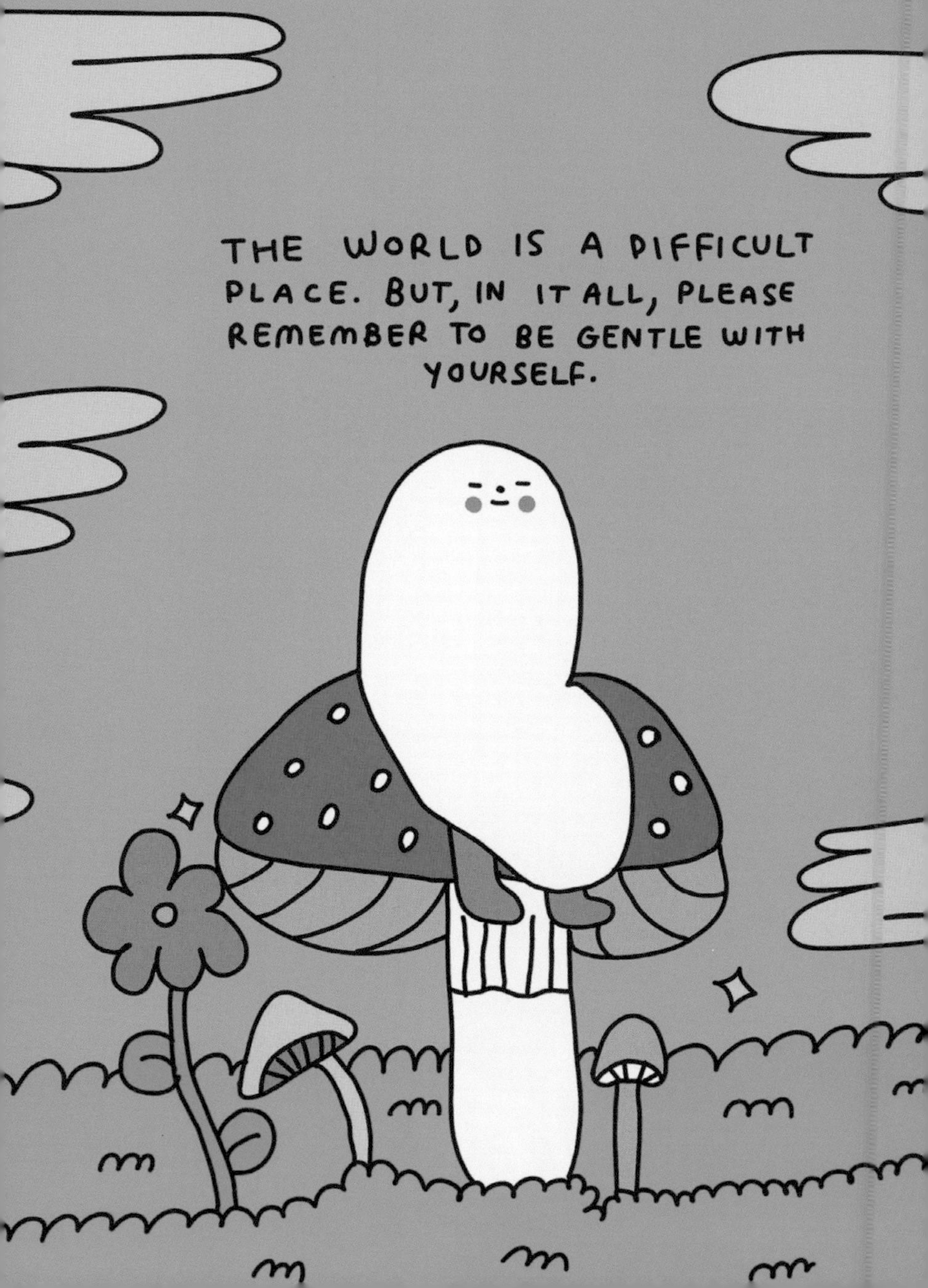
THE WORLD IS A DIFFICULT PLACE. BUT, IN IT ALL, PLEASE REMEMBER TO BE GENTLE WITH YOURSELF.

The world needs someone
like you in it.

So protect your energy fiercely.

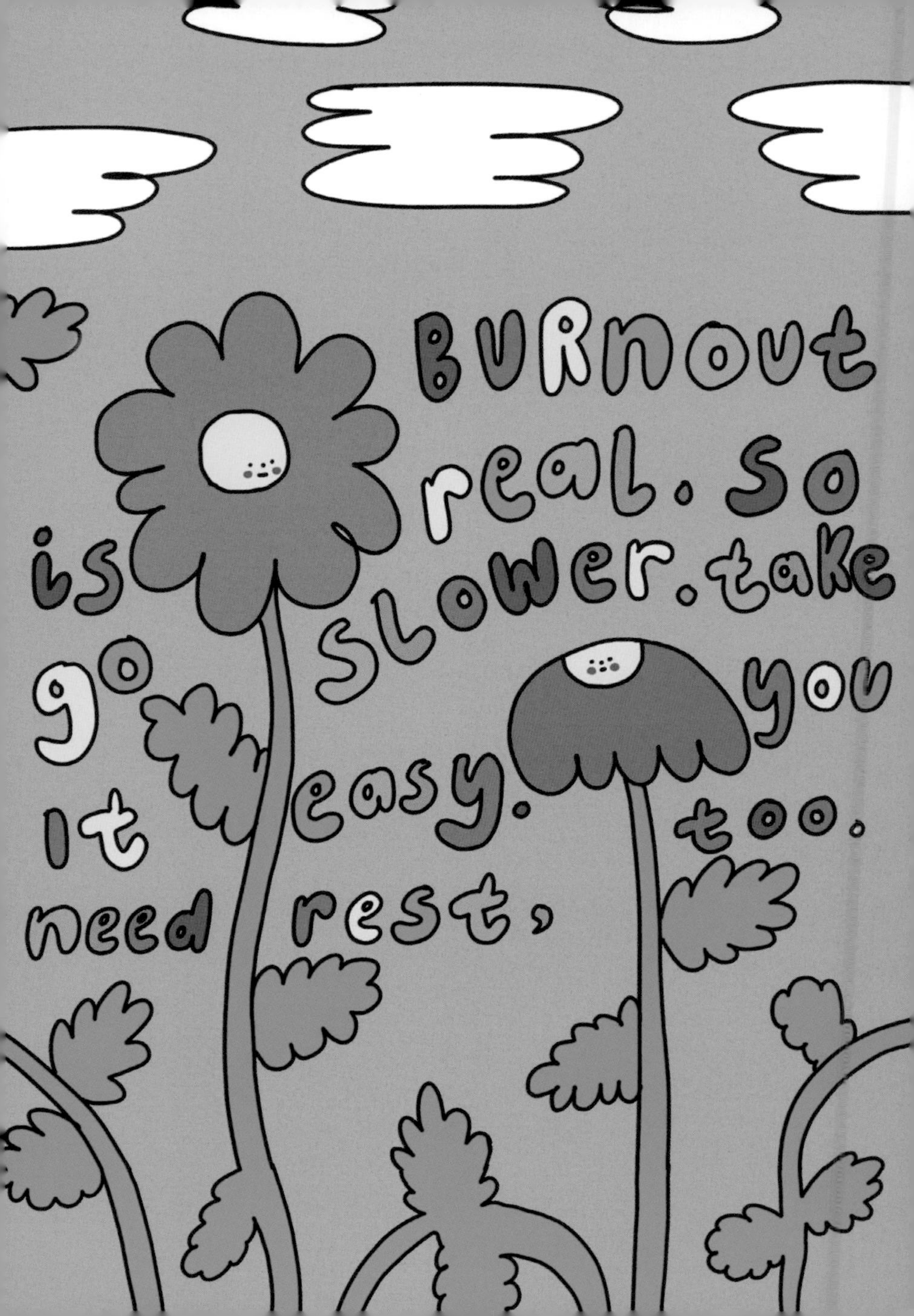
BURNOUT is real.
So go slower.
Take it easy.
You need rest, too.

You also deserve the love,
care and attention that you
give everyone else.

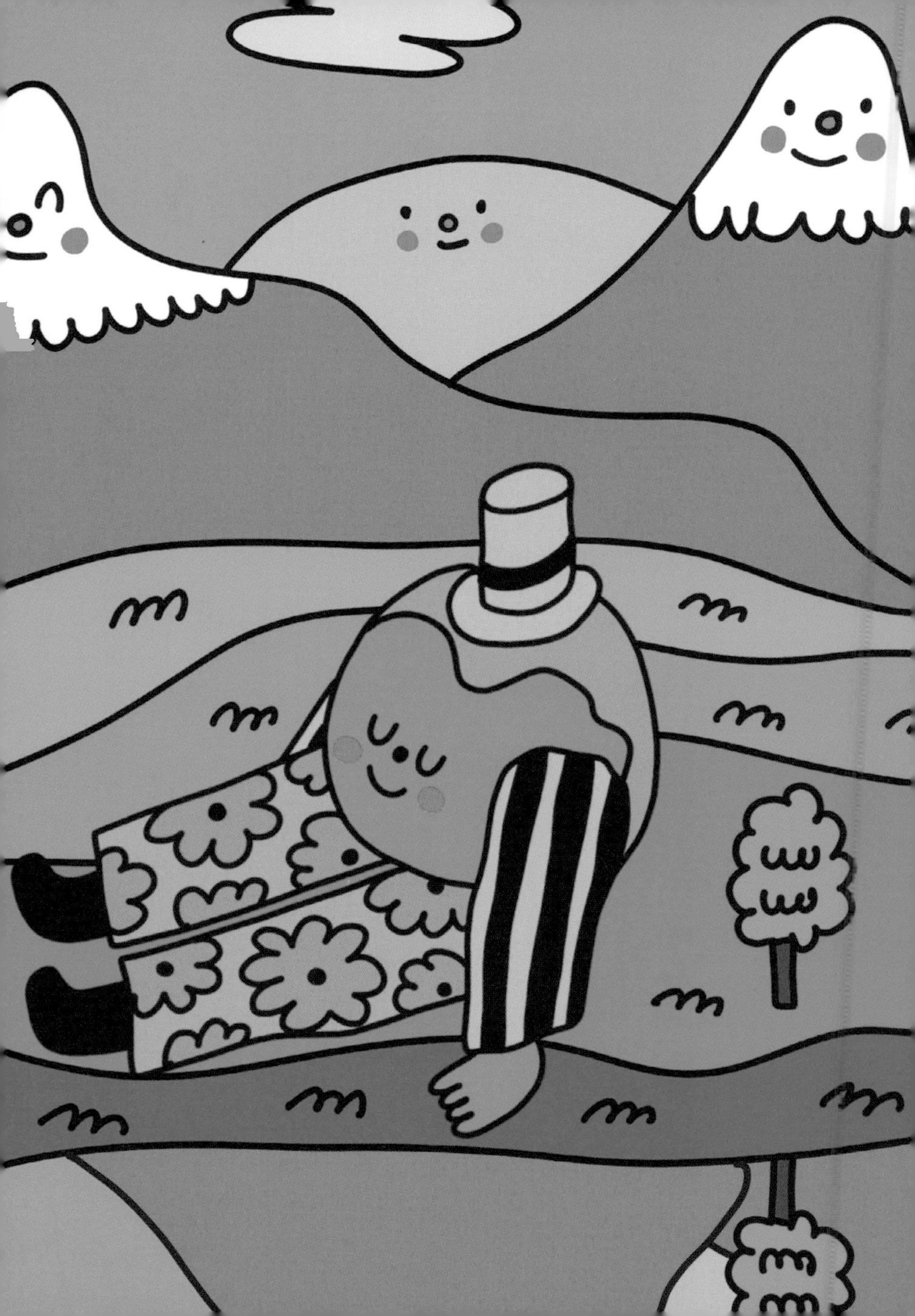

If you're feeling down right now, know that it is an appropriate response to the conditions we are living in. Be gentle with yourself.

If all you can do today is
survive, I'm proud of you.

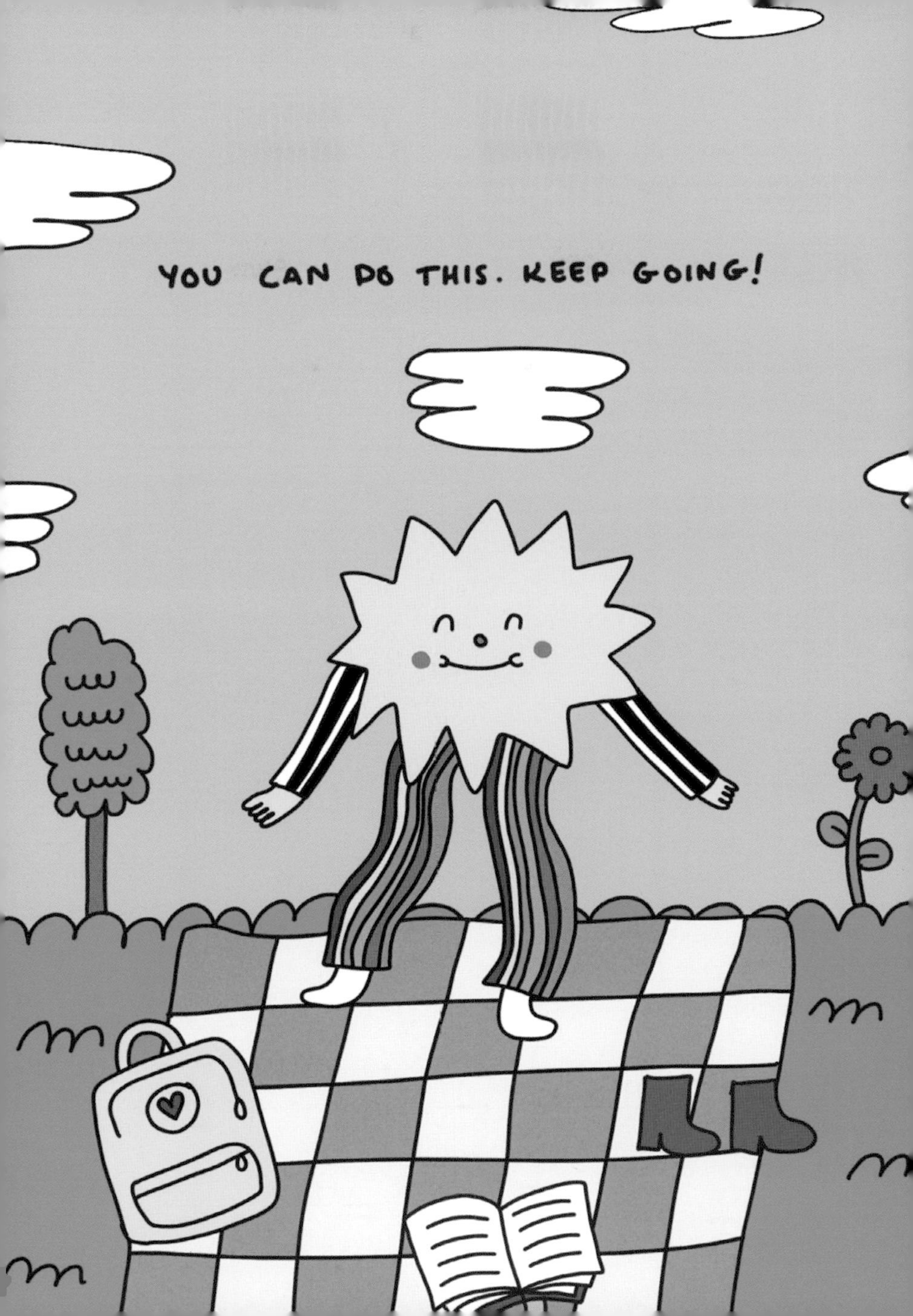
YOU CAN DO THIS. KEEP GOING!

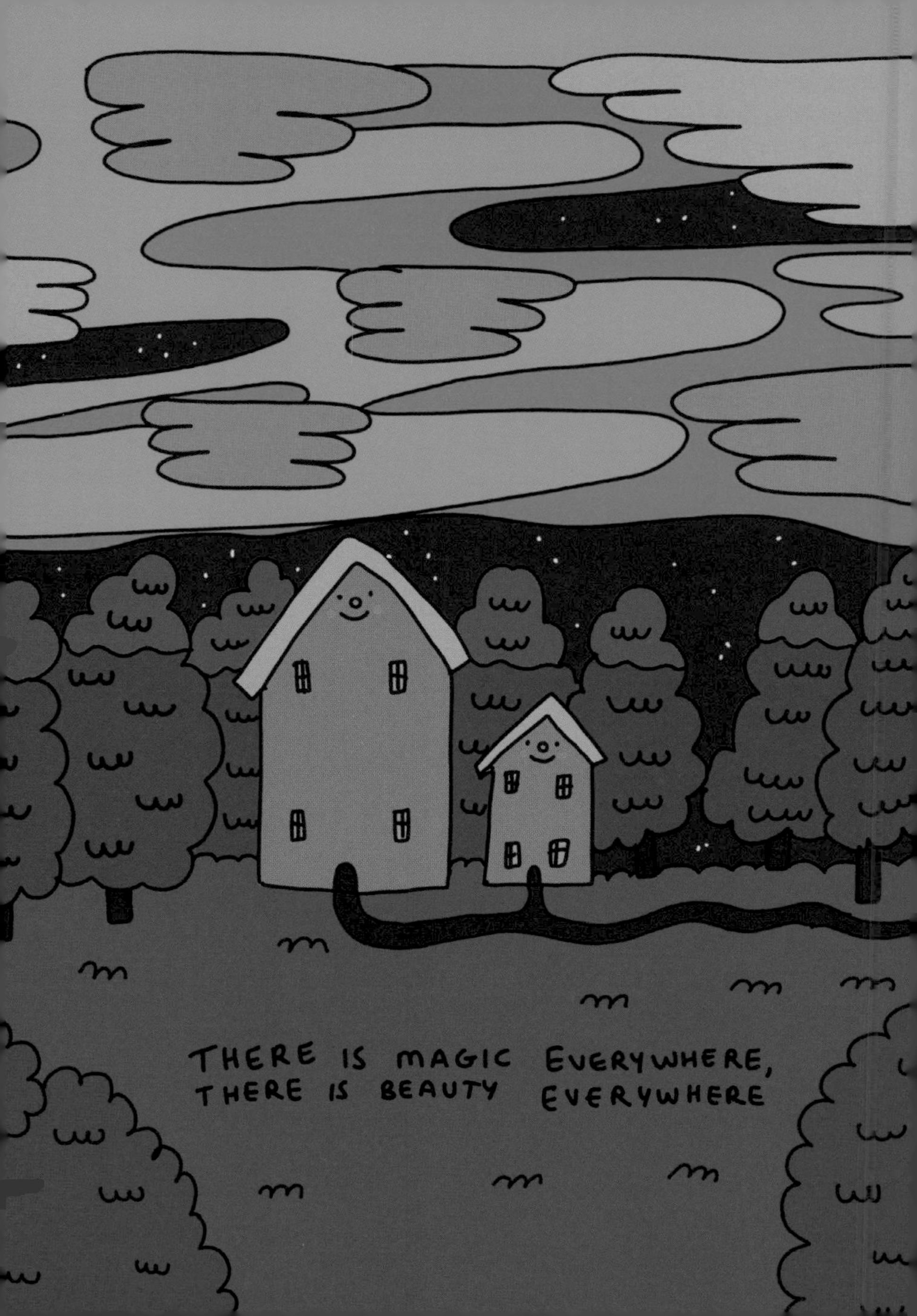
THERE IS MAGIC EVERYWHERE,
THERE IS BEAUTY EVERYWHERE

TODAY I INVITE ALL MAGIC INTO MY WORLD

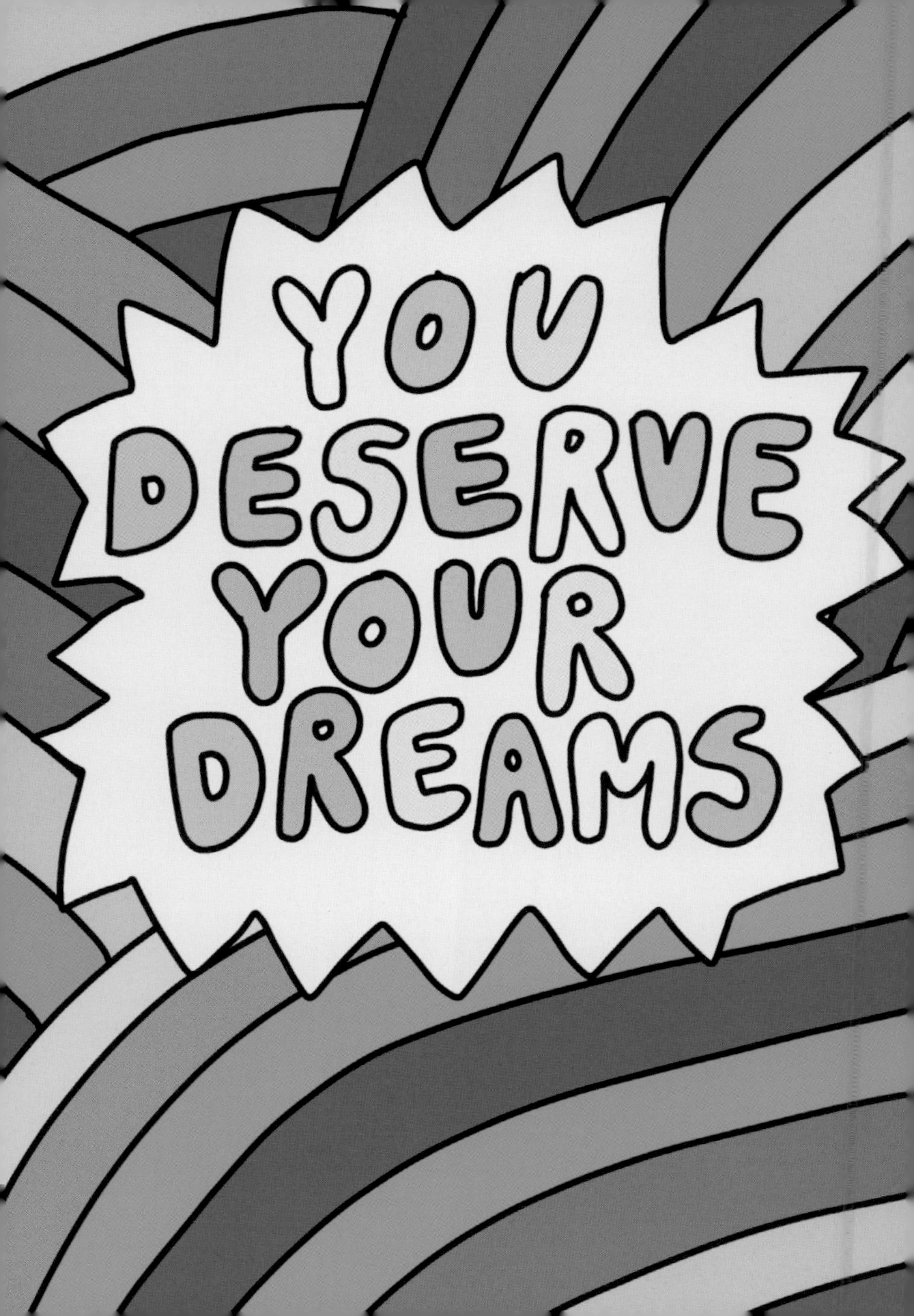
YOU DESERVE YOUR DREAMS

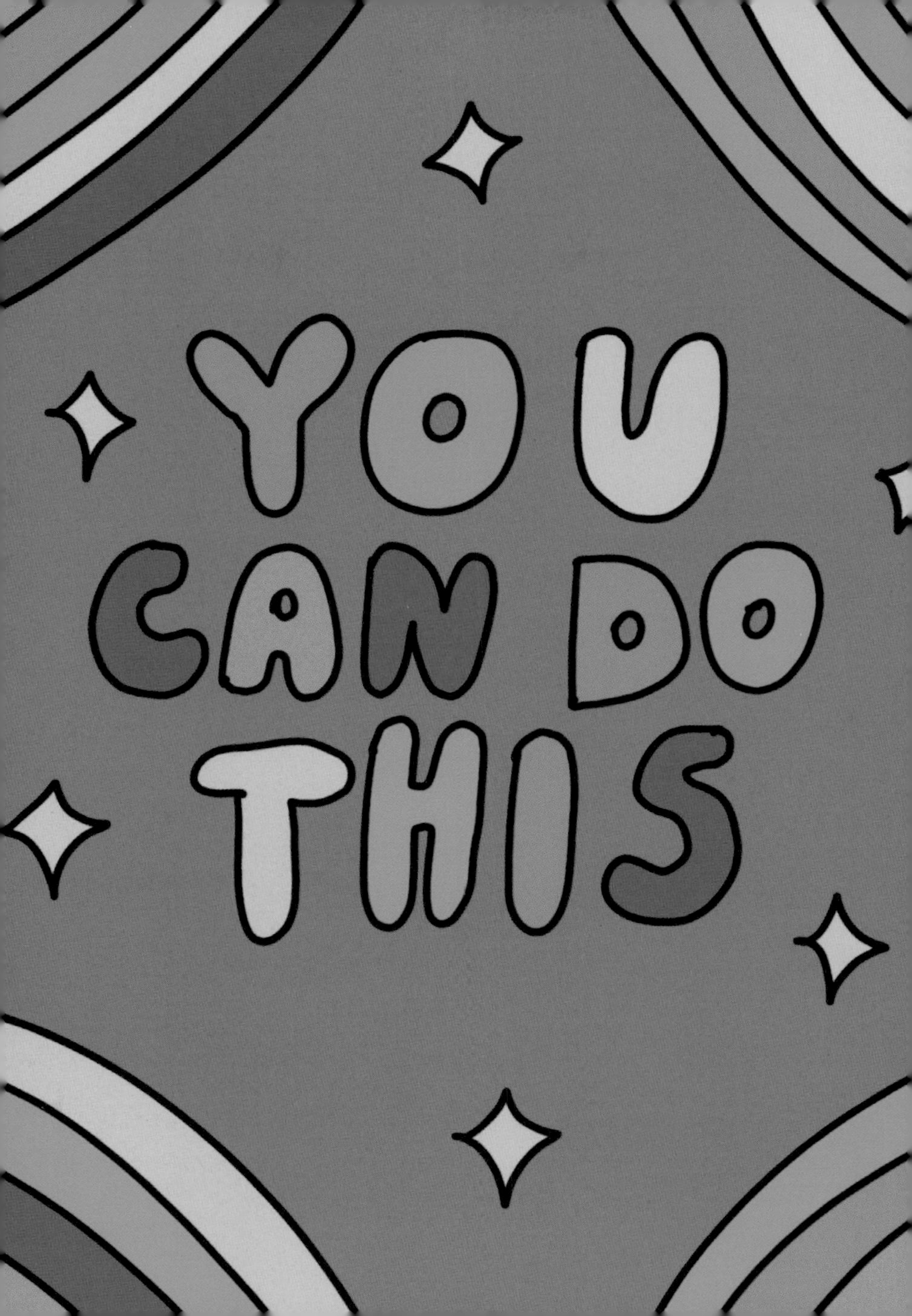
YOU
CAN DO
THIS

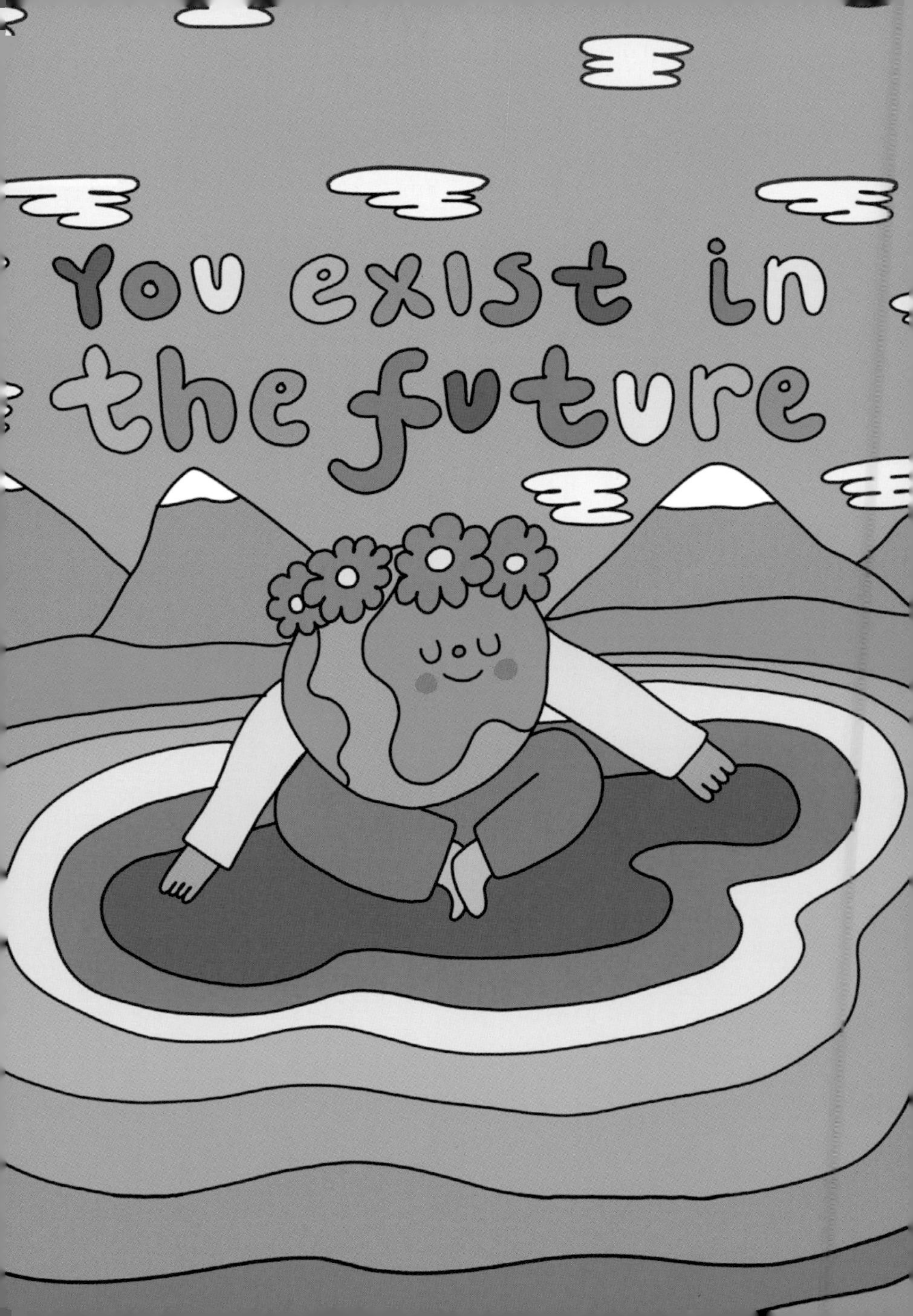
You exist in the future

The universe is guiding you.

CHANGE

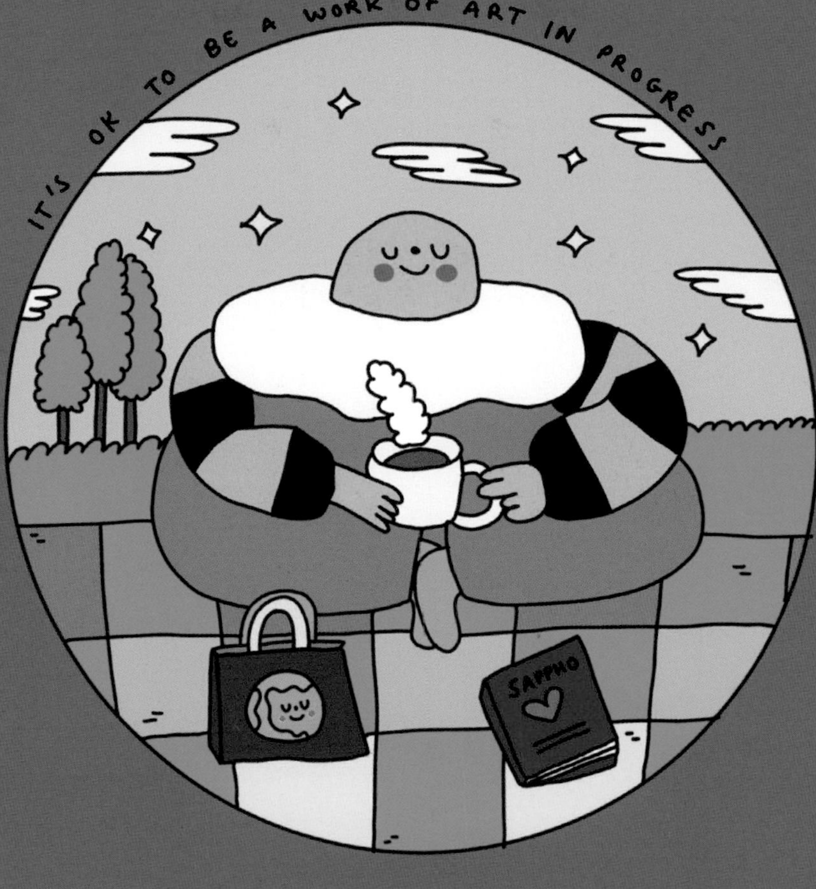
IT'S OK TO BE A WORK OF ART IN PROGRESS
SAPPHO

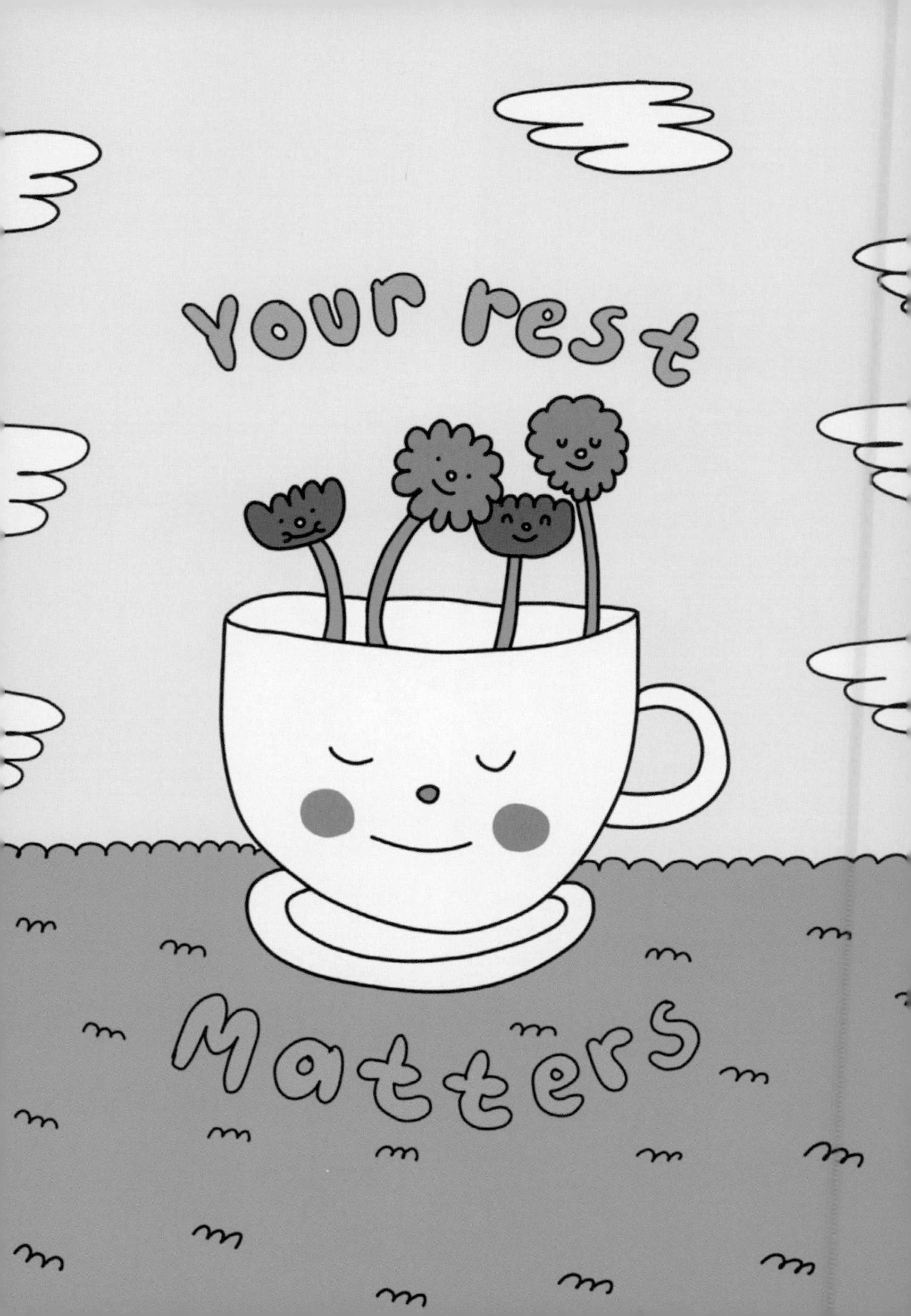
your rest
Matters

Change can be a challenge.

In all of it, remember to
recharge and take a moment
for yourself.

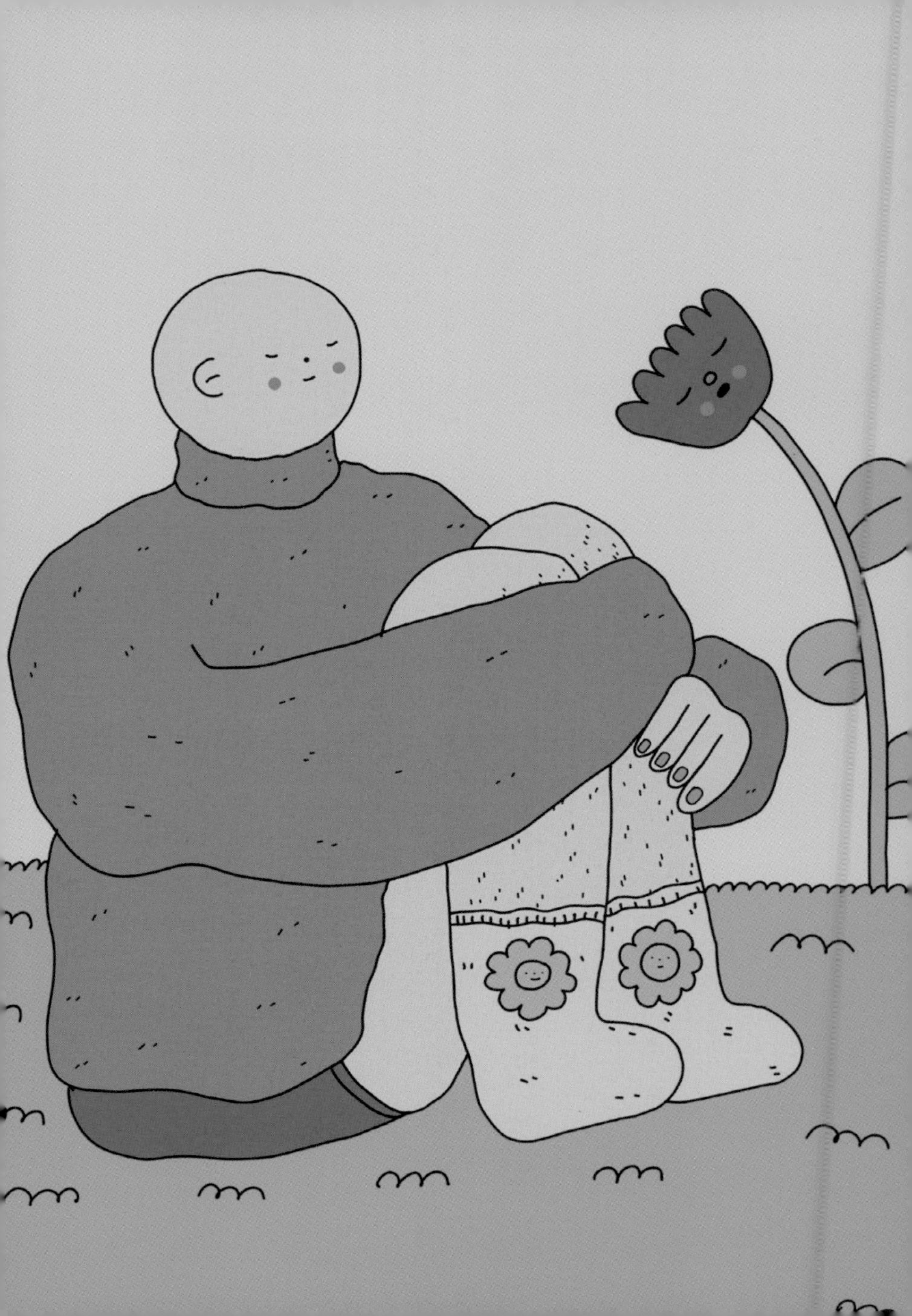

In the end, you'll stand up
and walk away, and that will
be the beginning.

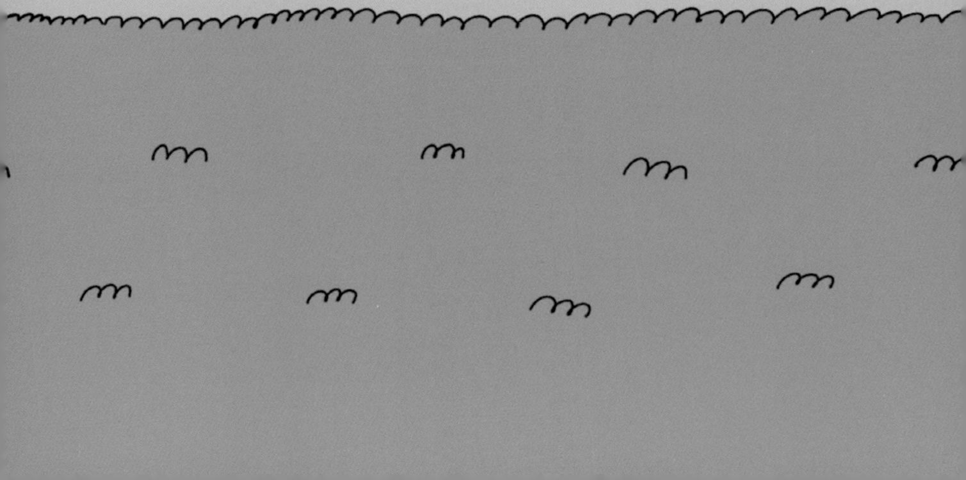

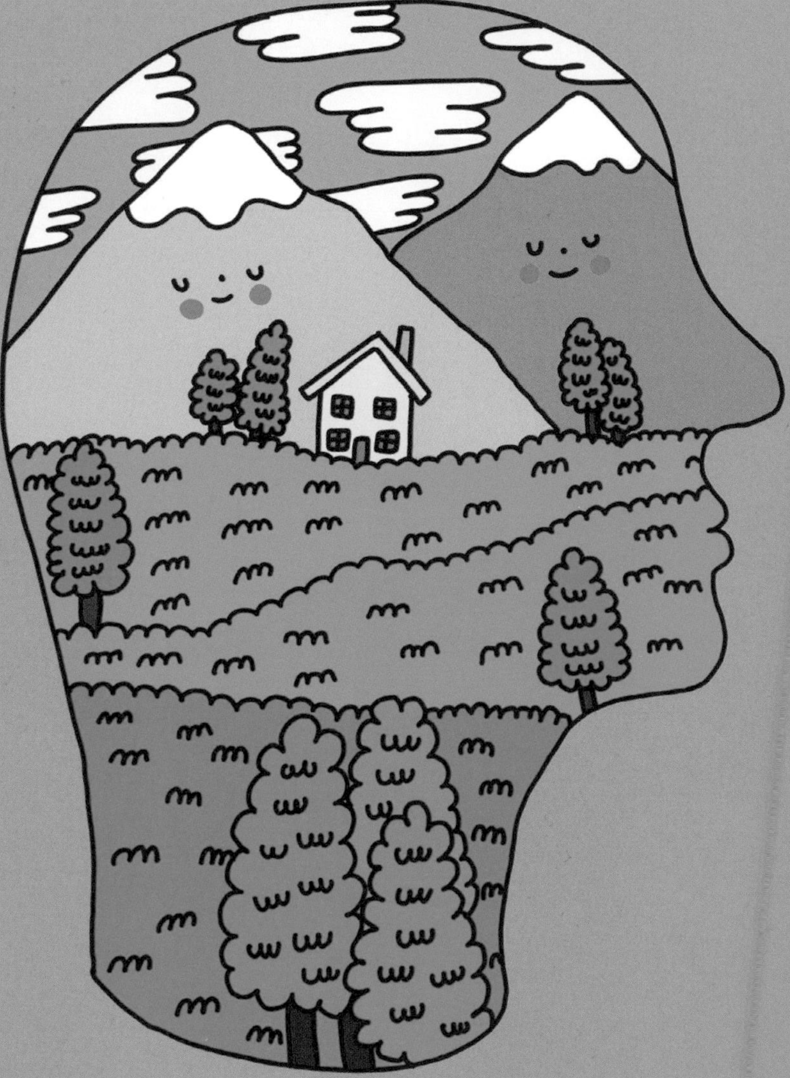

What would it look like if you stopped running and greeted home as a friend?

Breathe. Take a step forward
and know that this is the
beginning of a great journey.

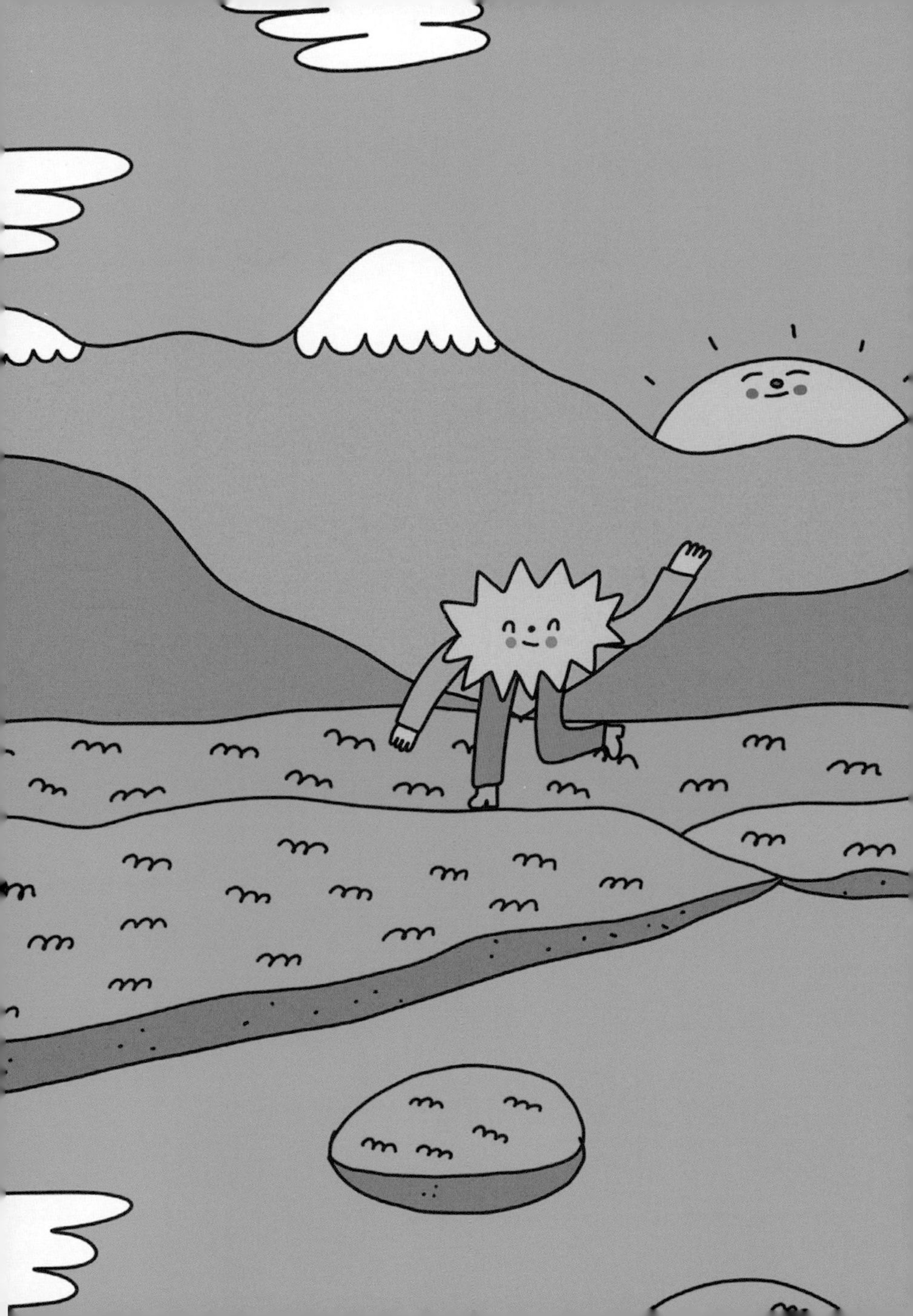

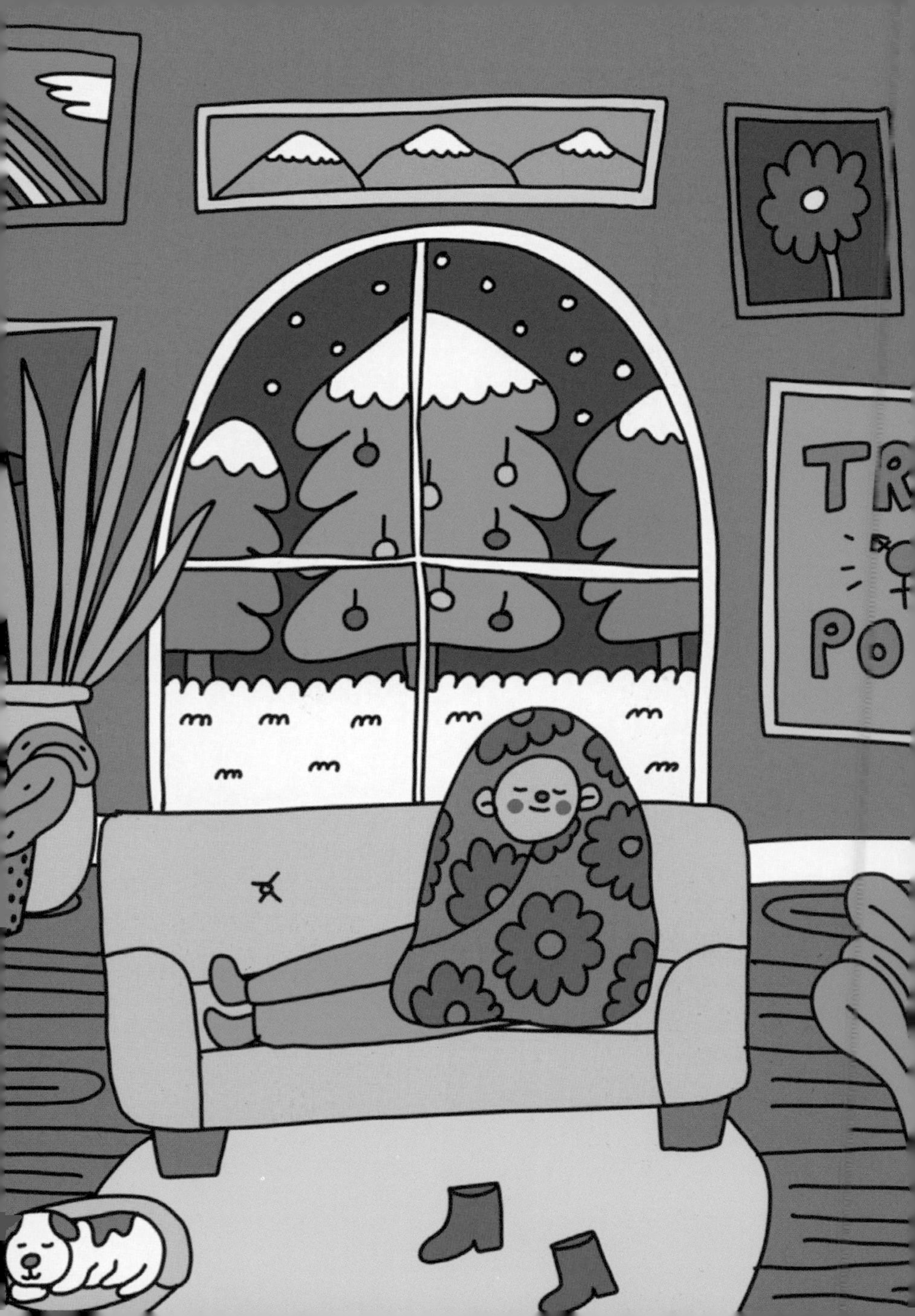

Forgive yourself for the mistakes you've made in the past. Embrace the person you are growing into.

Embrace the change,
keep moving forward.
There's a deep magic in
transition. You're moving
towards the light.

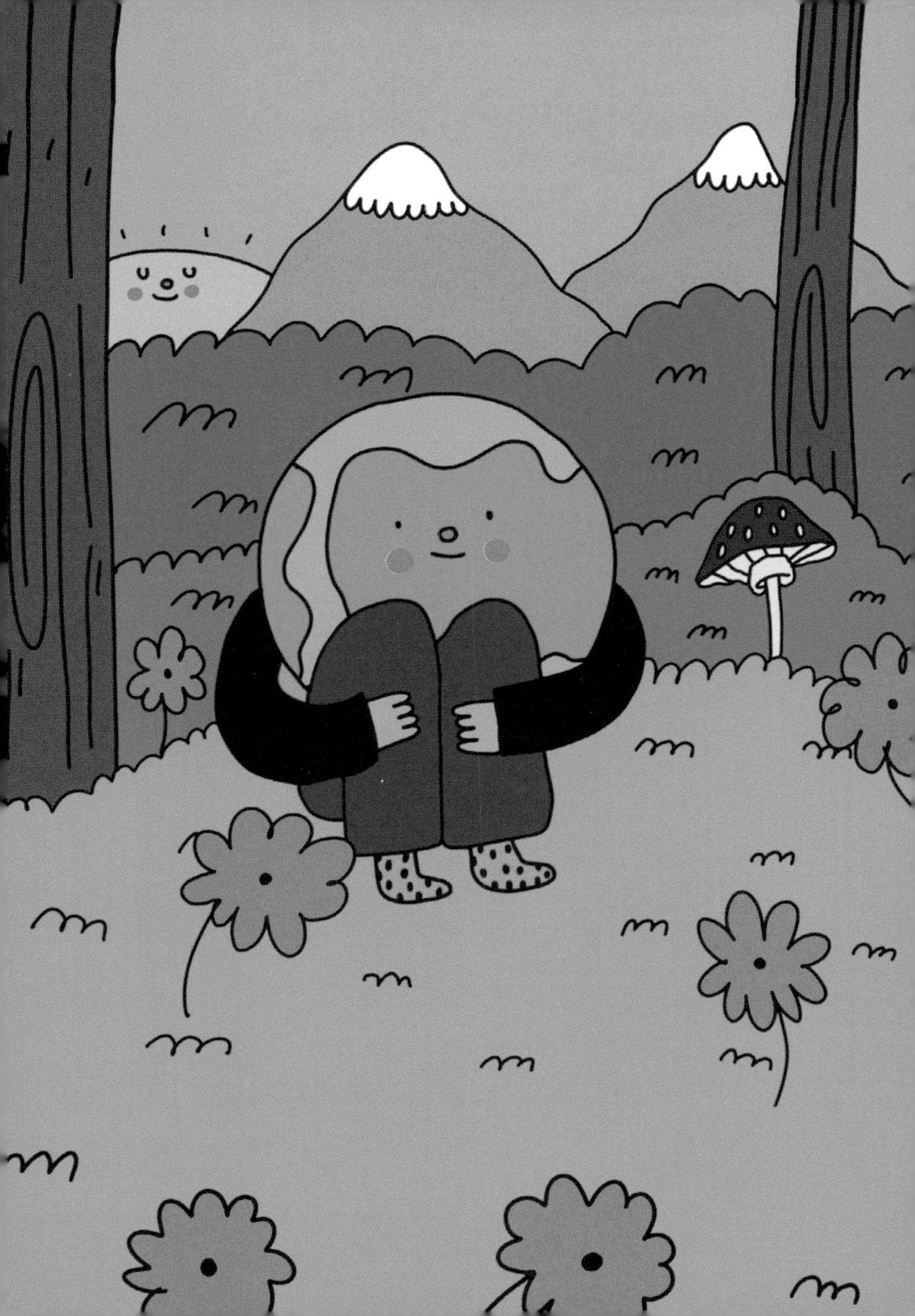

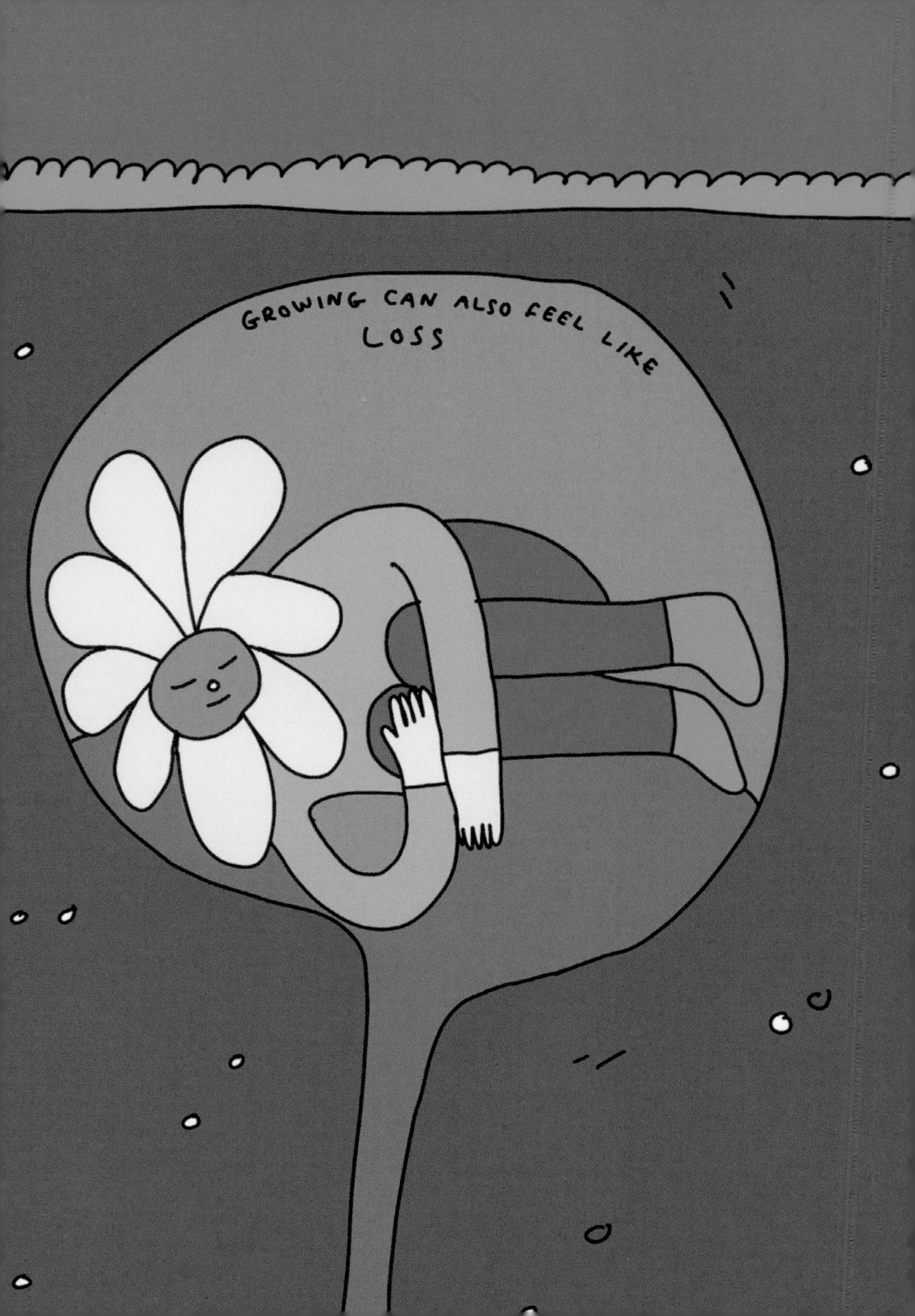
GROWING CAN ALSO FEEL LIKE
LOSS

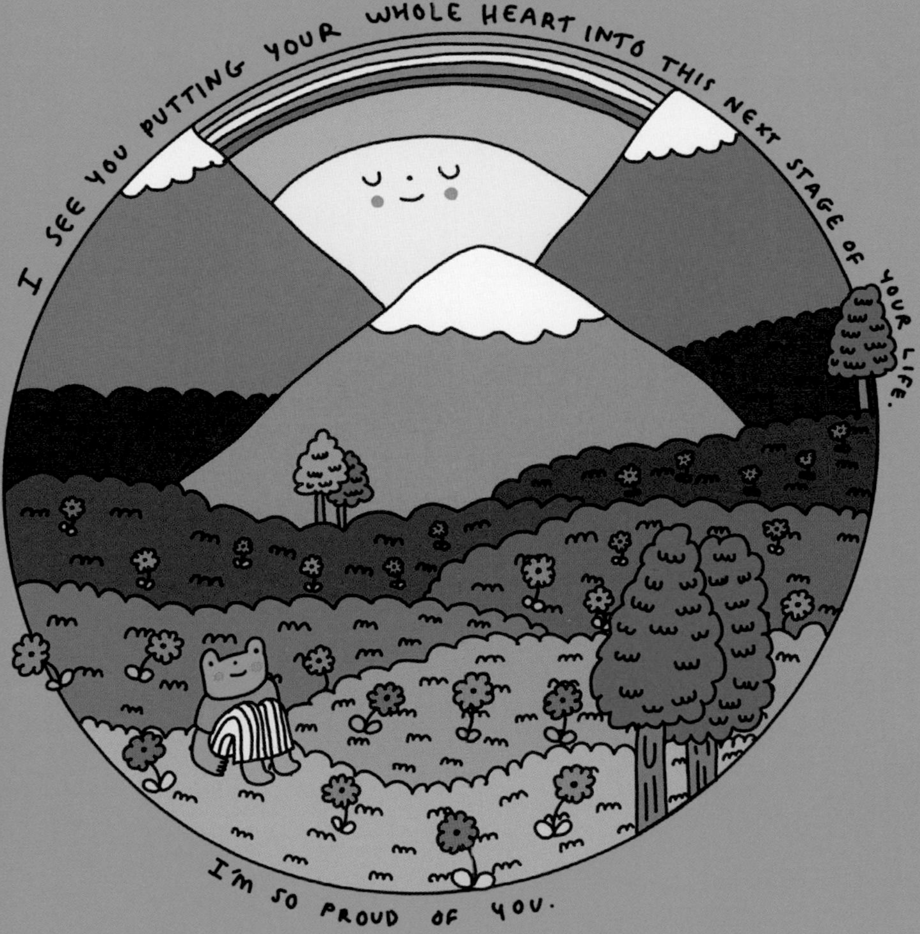
I SEE YOU PUTTING YOUR WHOLE HEART INTO THIS NEXT STAGE OF YOUR LIFE.
I'M SO PROUD OF YOU.

What if I told you to flow with the tide? Would you let go?

The river won't always feel smooth, but it will deliver you to your destination. May the torrents rock you. Surrender to the flow and feel the embrace of the universe.

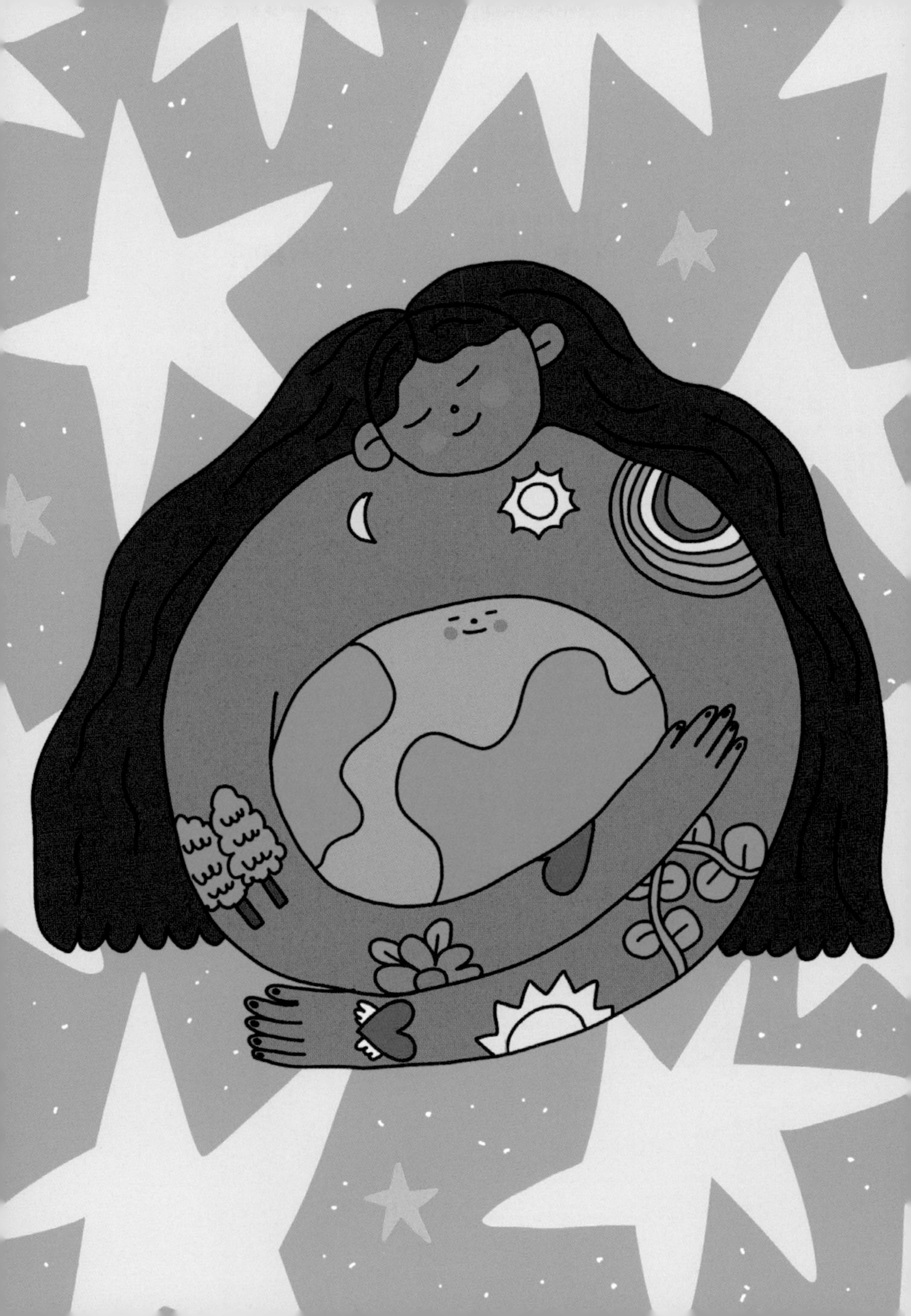

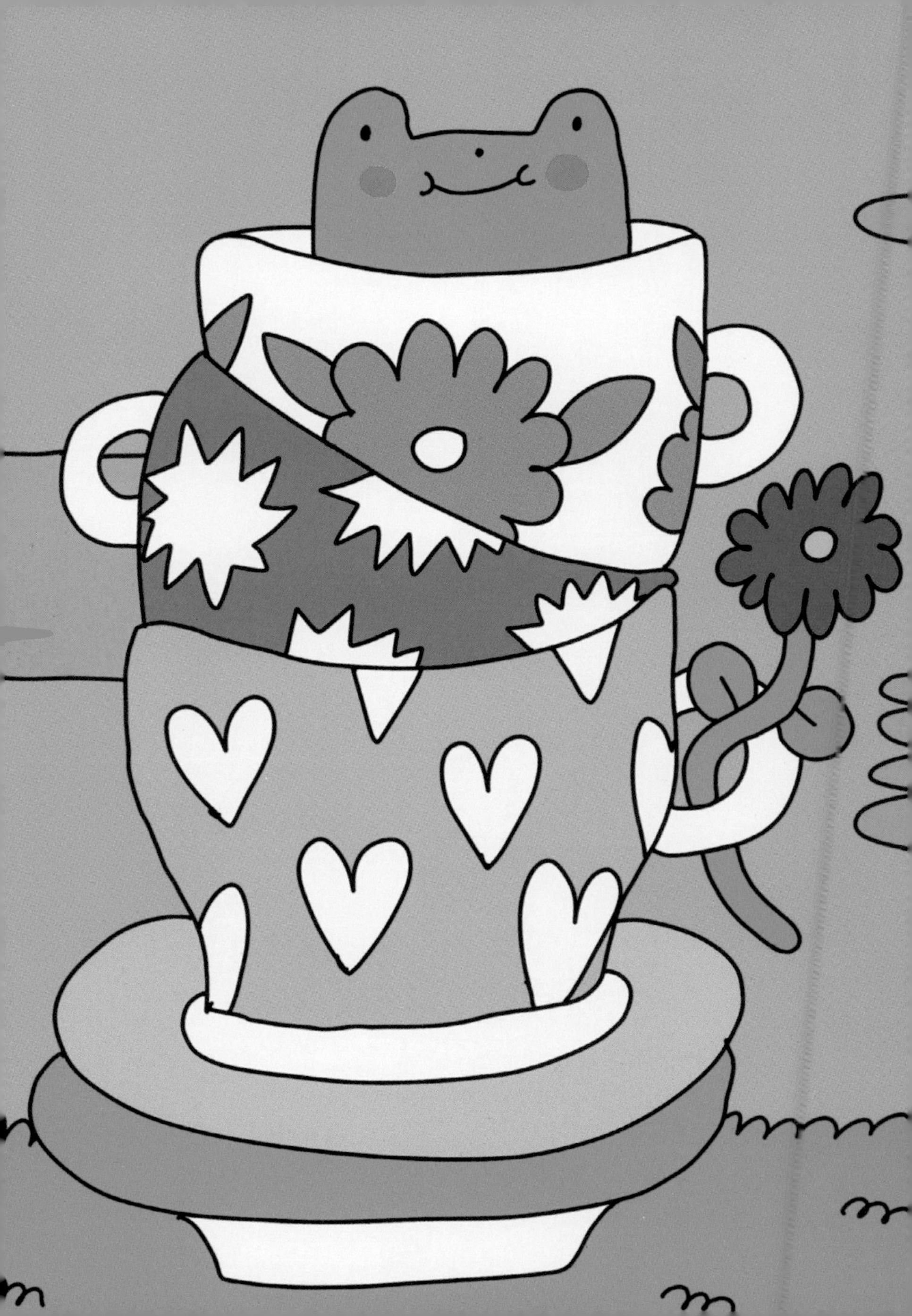

I see you navigating this change so gently. I'm proud of you for staying true to yourself amid the stress.

Remember when you
dreamed of being where
you are now.

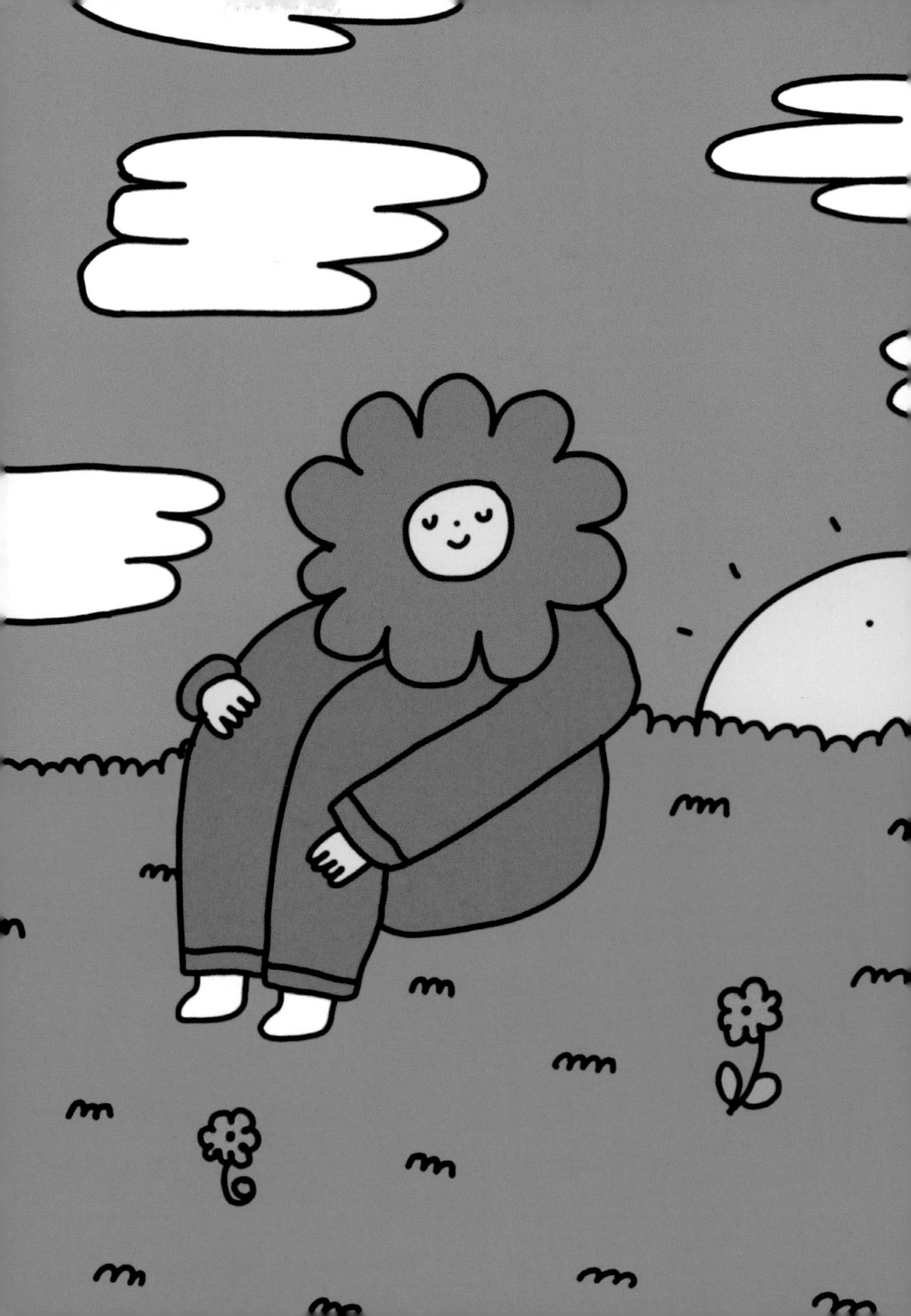

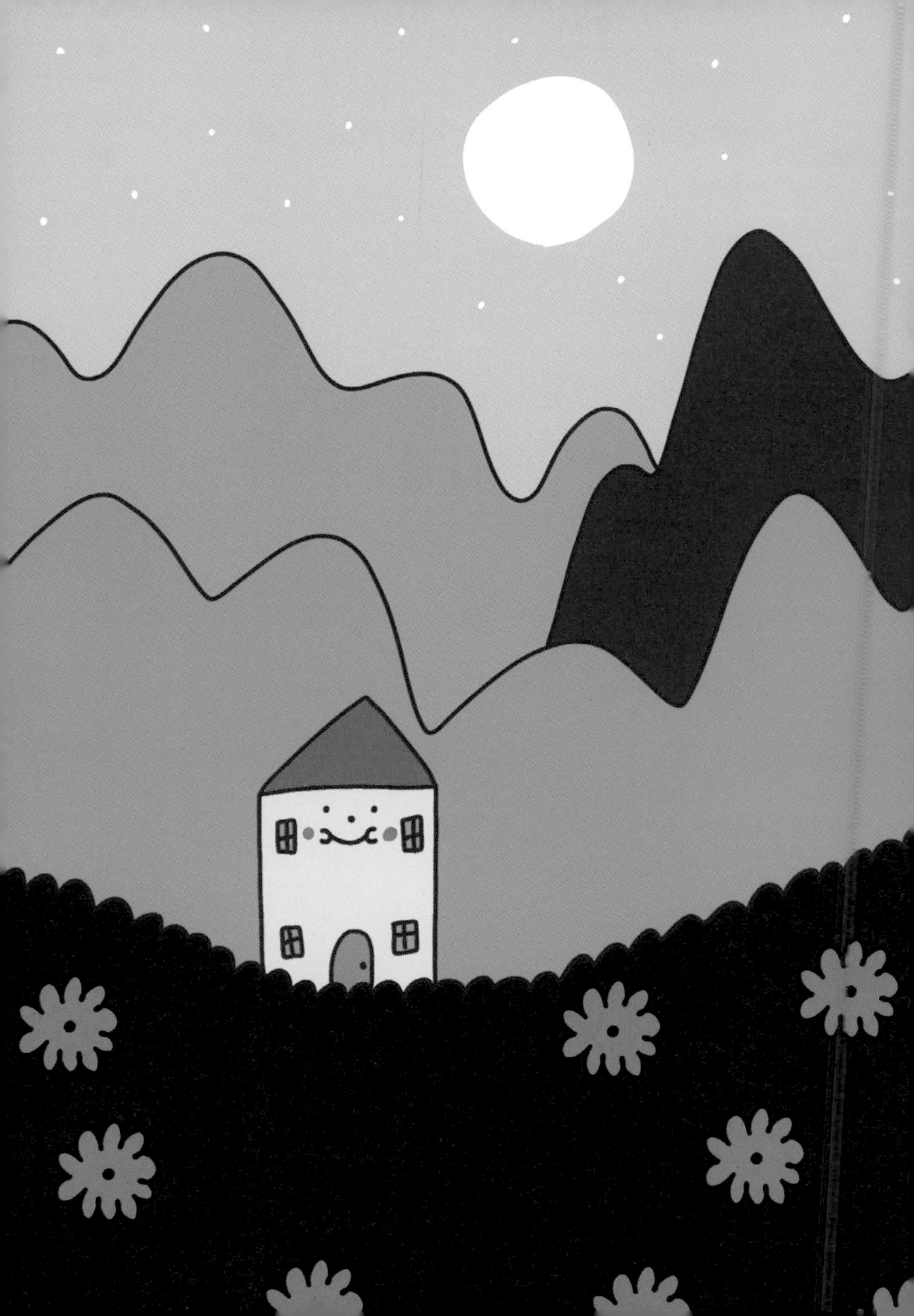

Trust that the light is coming
to show you that you are right
where you are meant to be.

When this new wave reaches
the shore, take time to find
yourself again and again
and again.

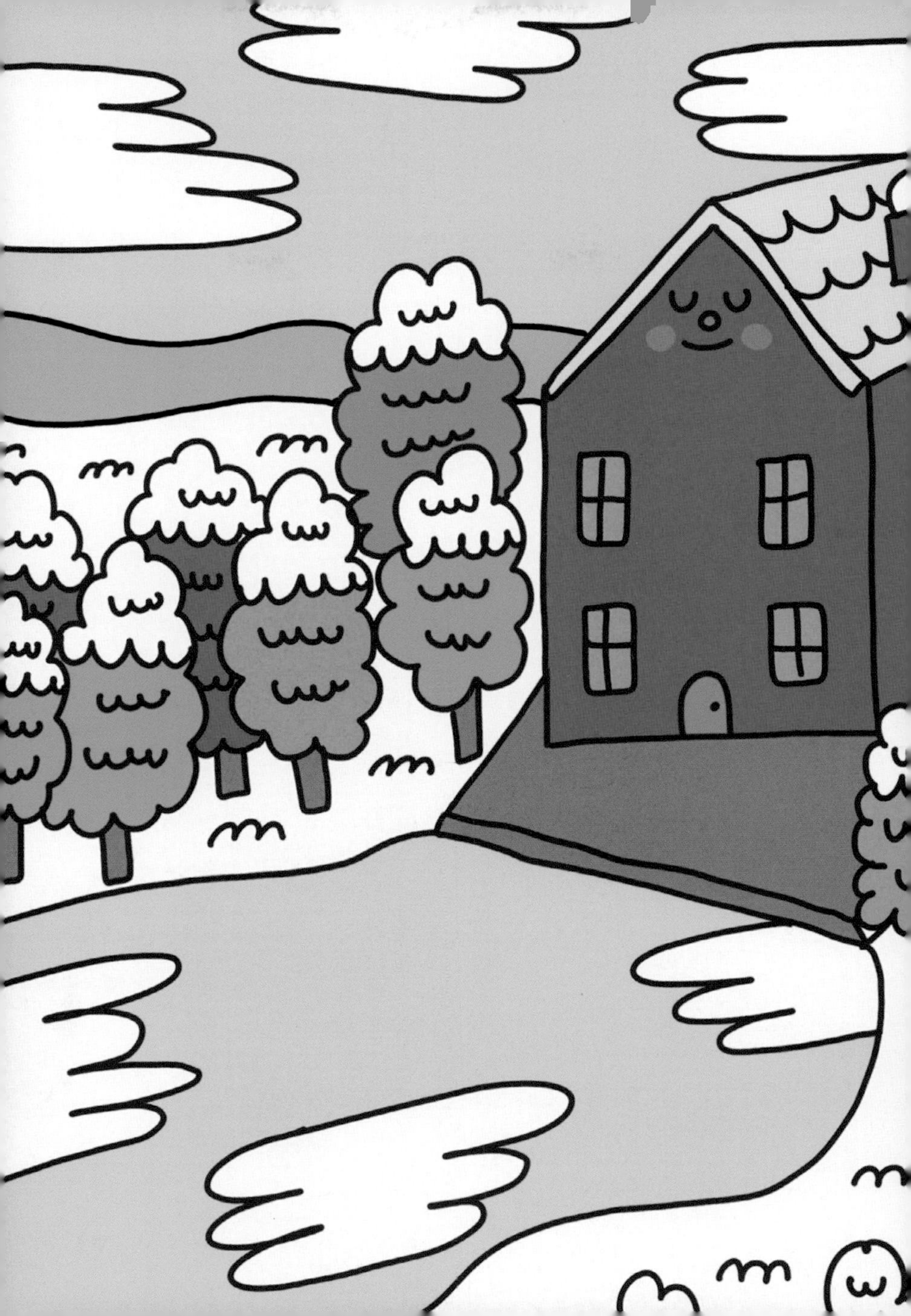

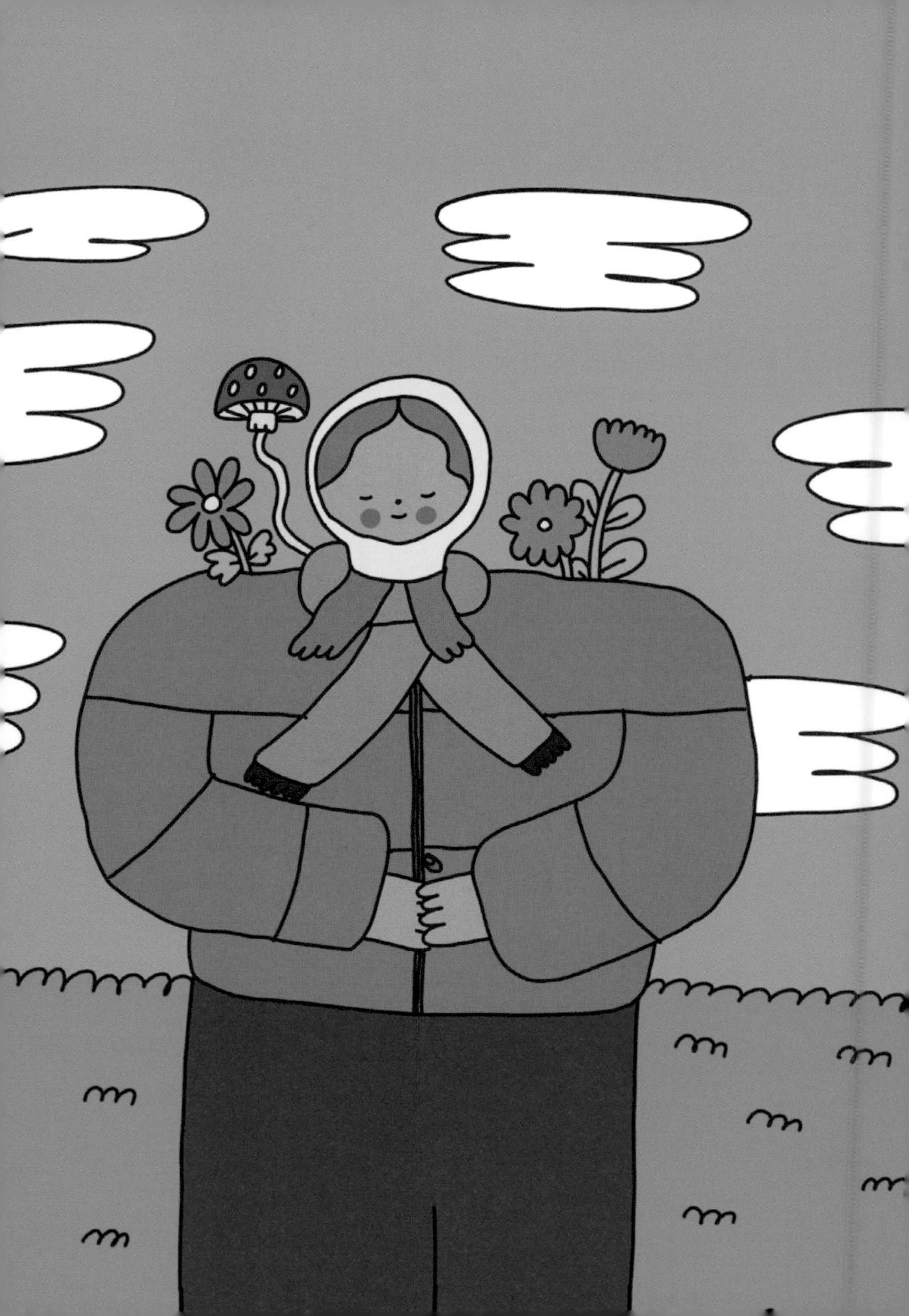

I realise that I'm not
scared of changing any more,
I'm scared of staying the same.

I SEE YOU

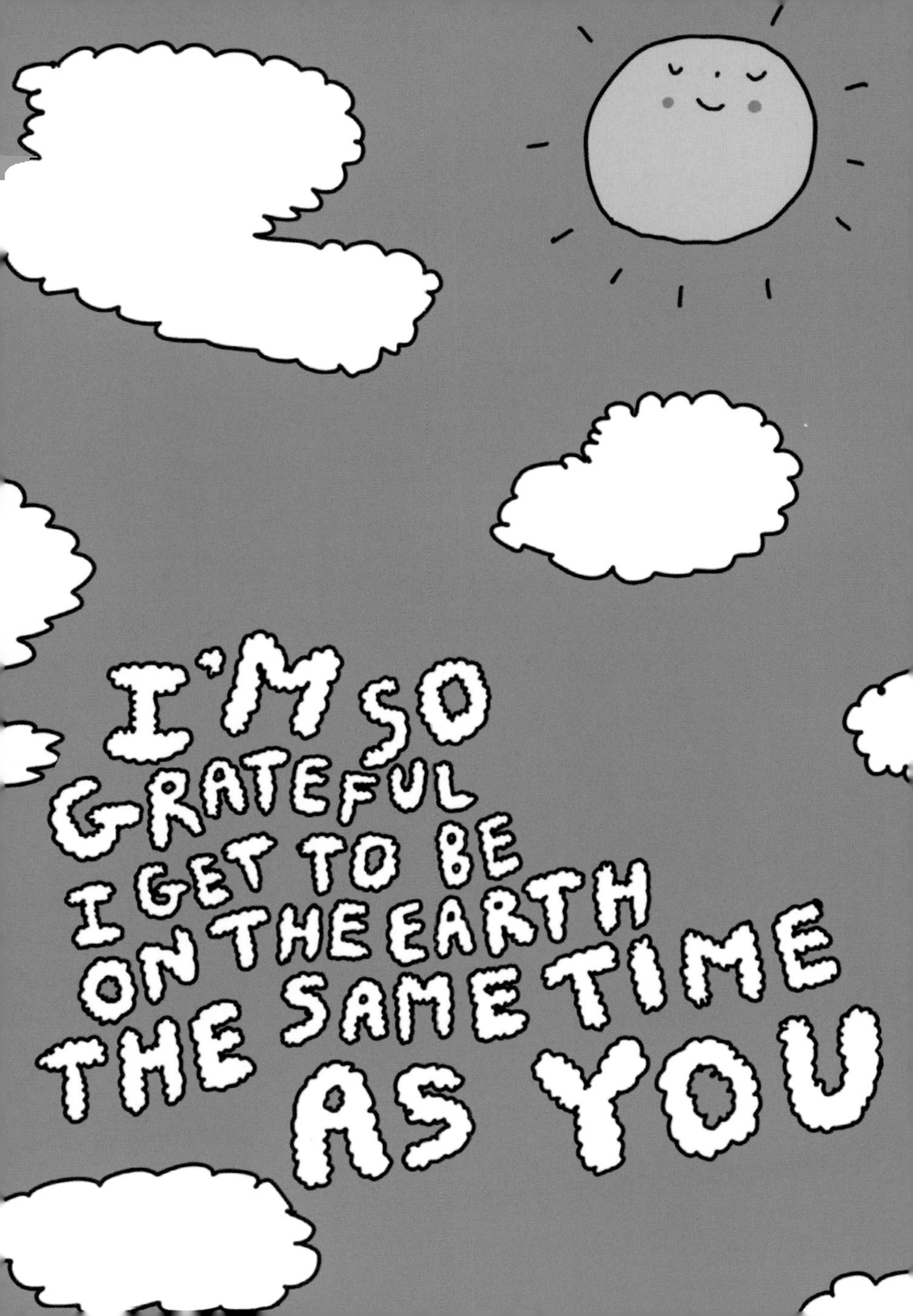
I'M SO GRATEFUL I GET TO BE ON THE EARTH THE SAME TIME AS YOU

IT'S GOOD TO SEE YOU TAKING SPACE FOR YOURSELF AFTER SO LONG IN SURVIVAL MODE. YOU'RE DOING SO WELL. YESTERDAY'S AND THE FUTURE YOU ARE SO PROUD OF YOU.

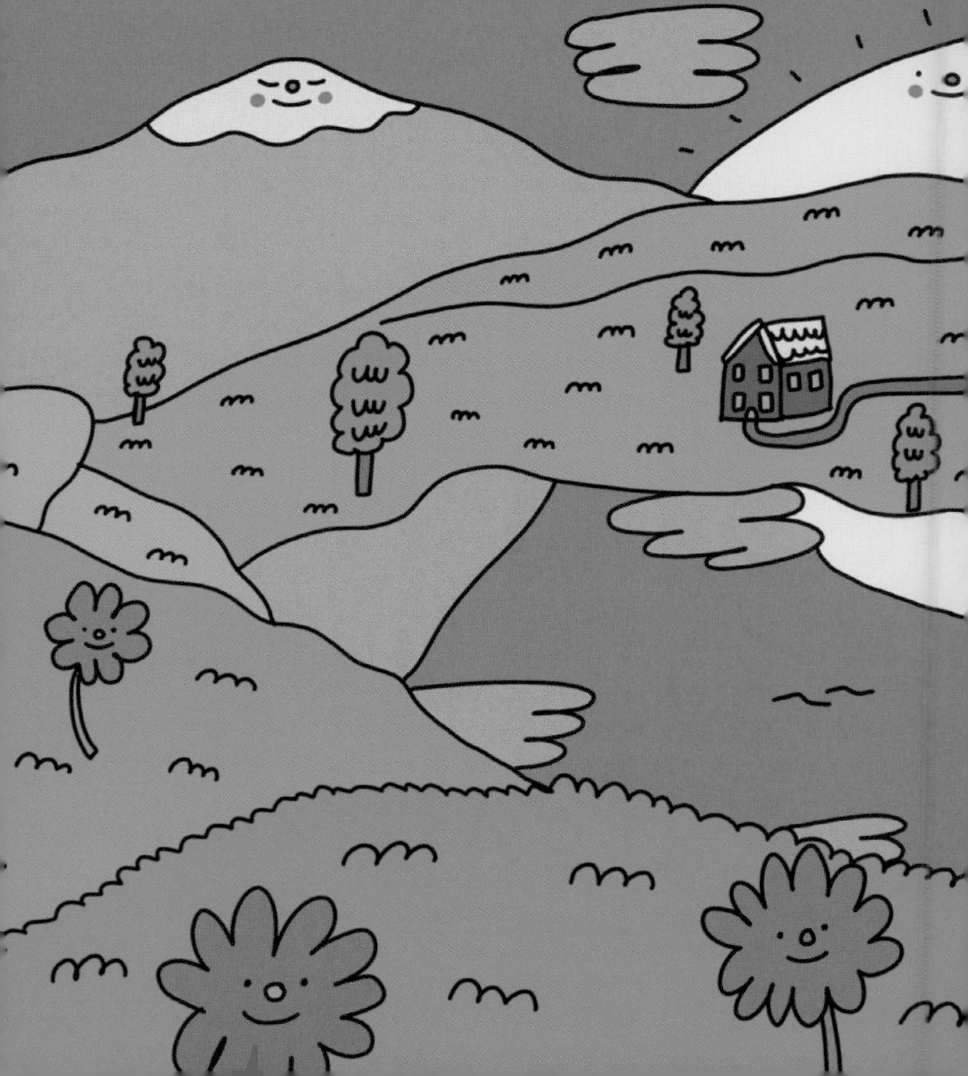

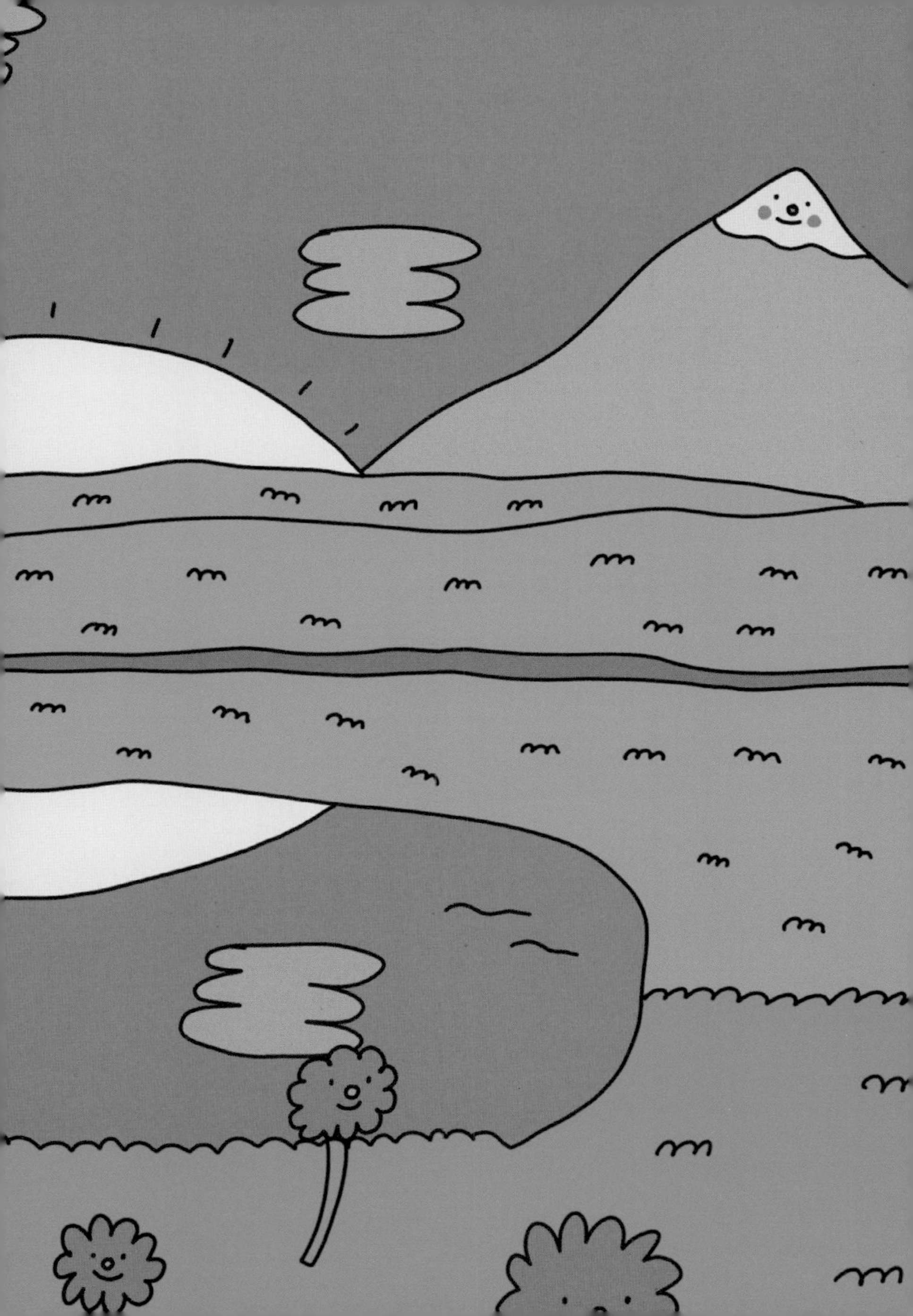

I see you moving out
of your own way.

I see you moving out of the
shadow and into the light.

And God,
do you deserve the light.

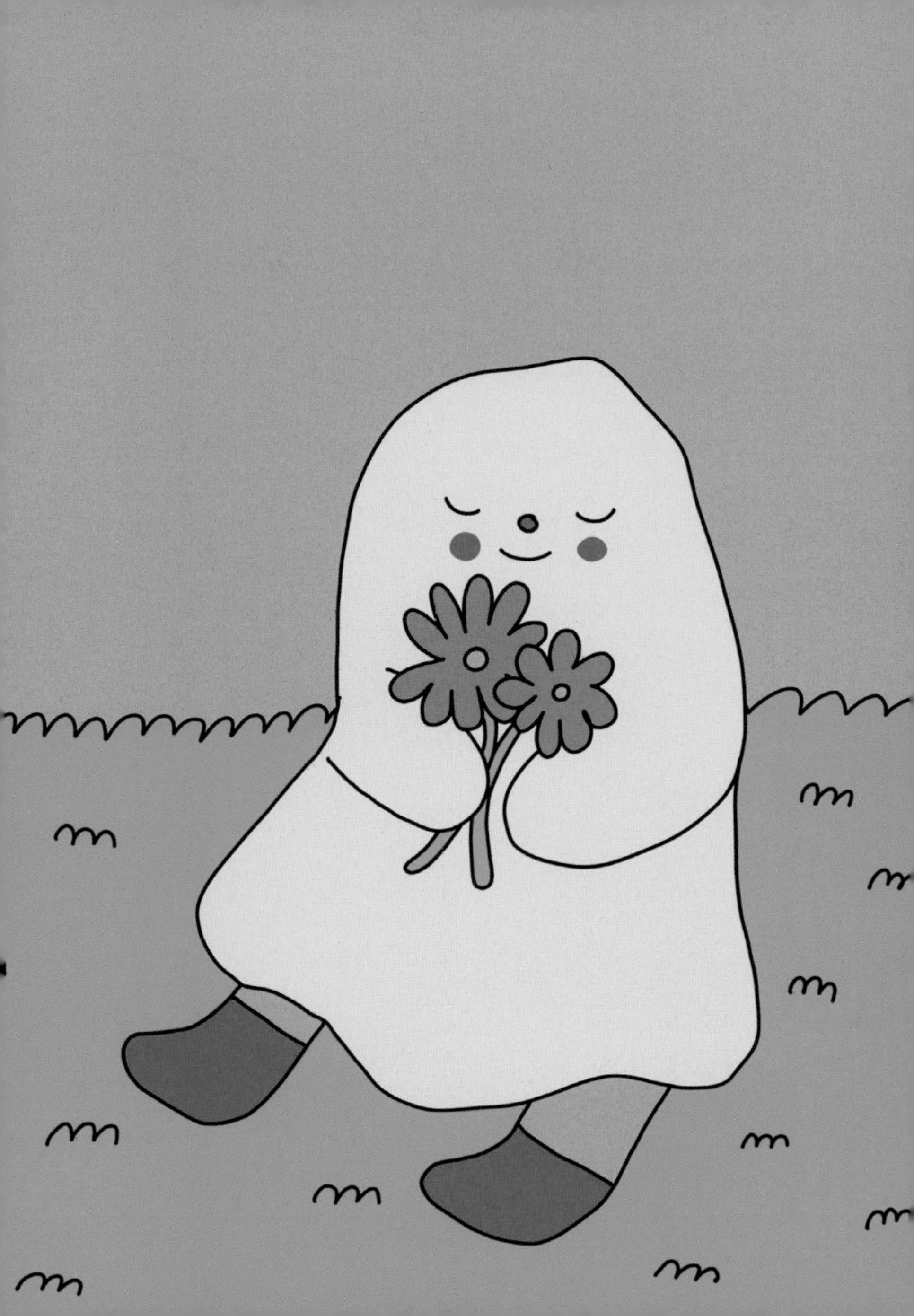

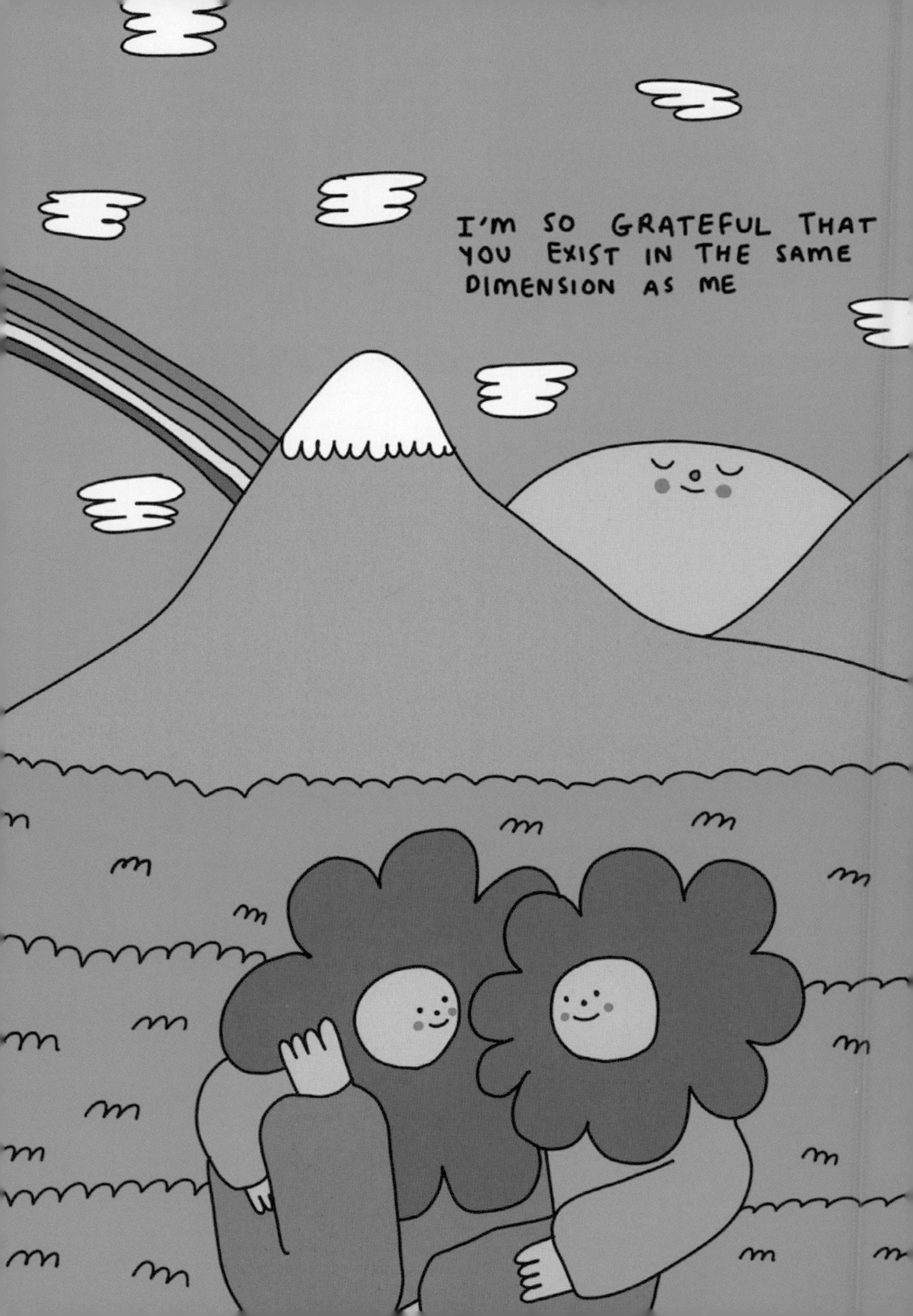
I'M SO GRATEFUL THAT YOU EXIST IN THE SAME DIMENSION AS ME

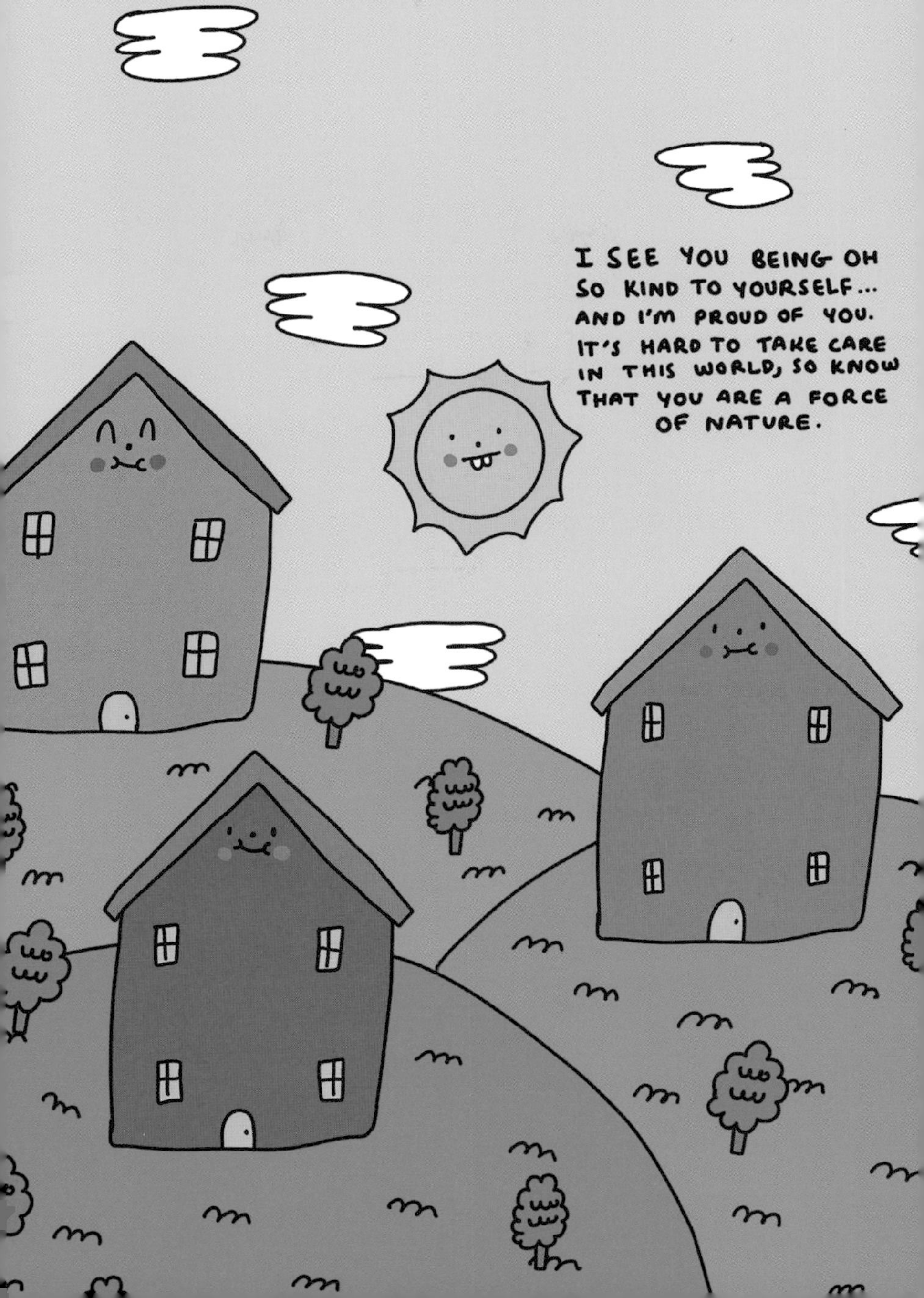
I SEE YOU BEING OH SO KIND TO YOURSELF... AND I'M PROUD OF YOU. IT'S HARD TO TAKE CARE IN THIS WORLD, SO KNOW THAT YOU ARE A FORCE OF NATURE.

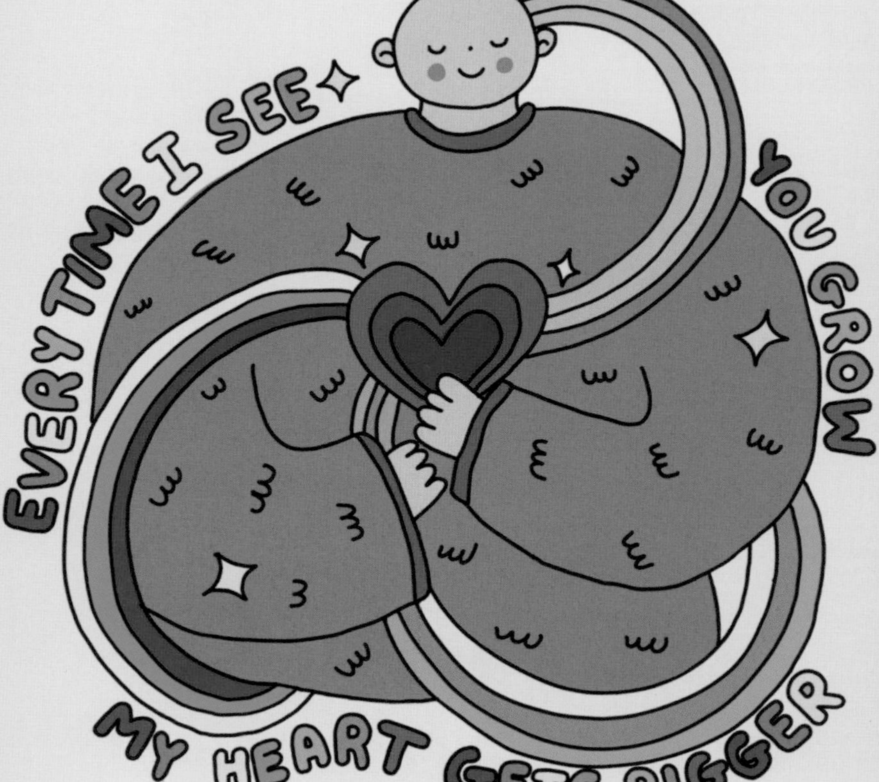
EVERY TIME I SEE YOU GROW
MY HEART GETS BIGGER

I see you making space for
your own growth, and wanted
to tell you that your courage
is so inspiring to me.

You are a total force of nature.

I SEE YOU TAKING UP MORE SPACE FOR YOURSELF. I SEE YOU DARING TO DREAM AND LOVE AND GROW

THE WORLD IS TRULY A MAGICAL PLACE WITH YOU IN IT!

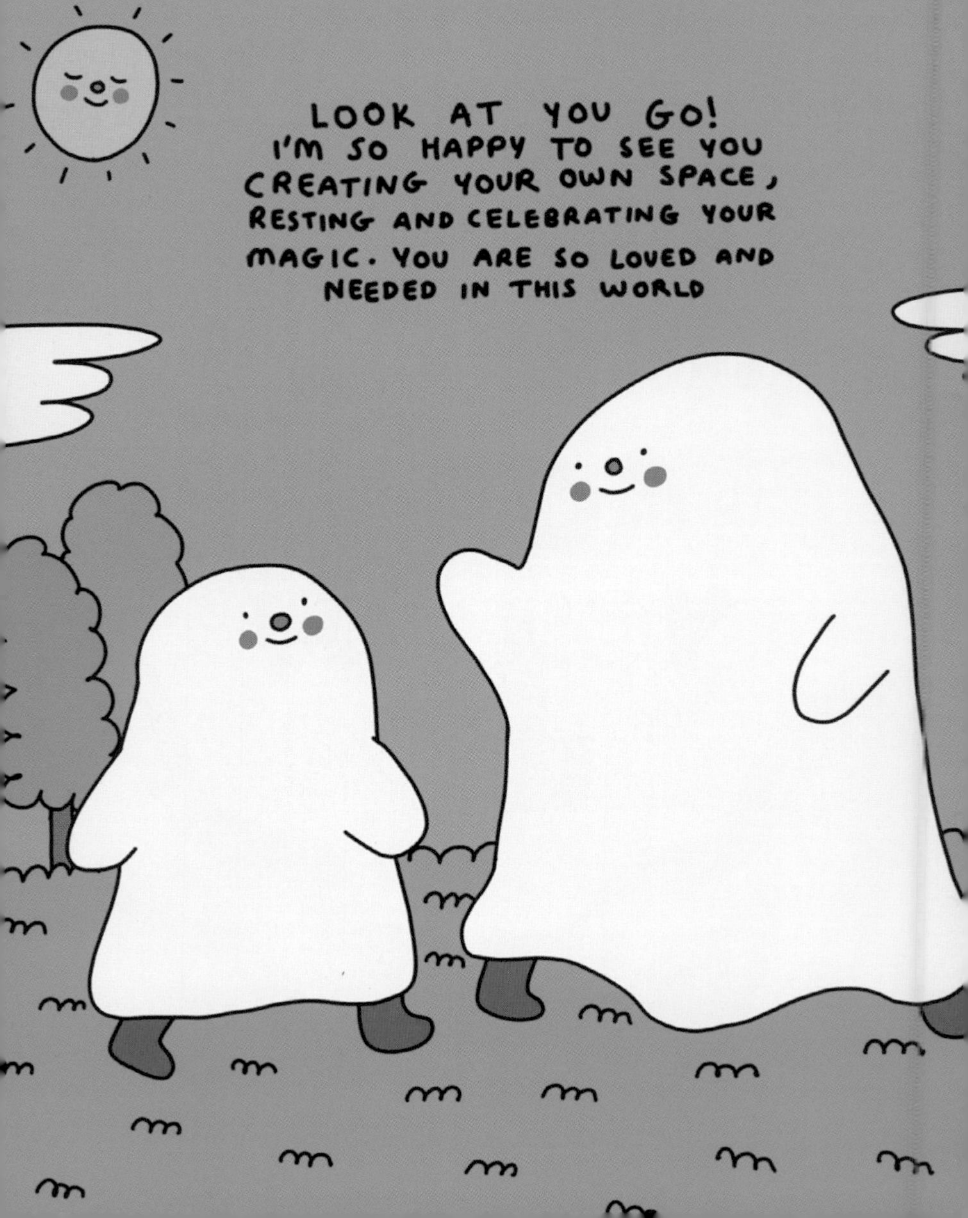
LOOK AT YOU GO!
I'M SO HAPPY TO SEE YOU CREATING YOUR OWN SPACE, RESTING AND CELEBRATING YOUR MAGIC. YOU ARE SO LOVED AND NEEDED IN THIS WORLD

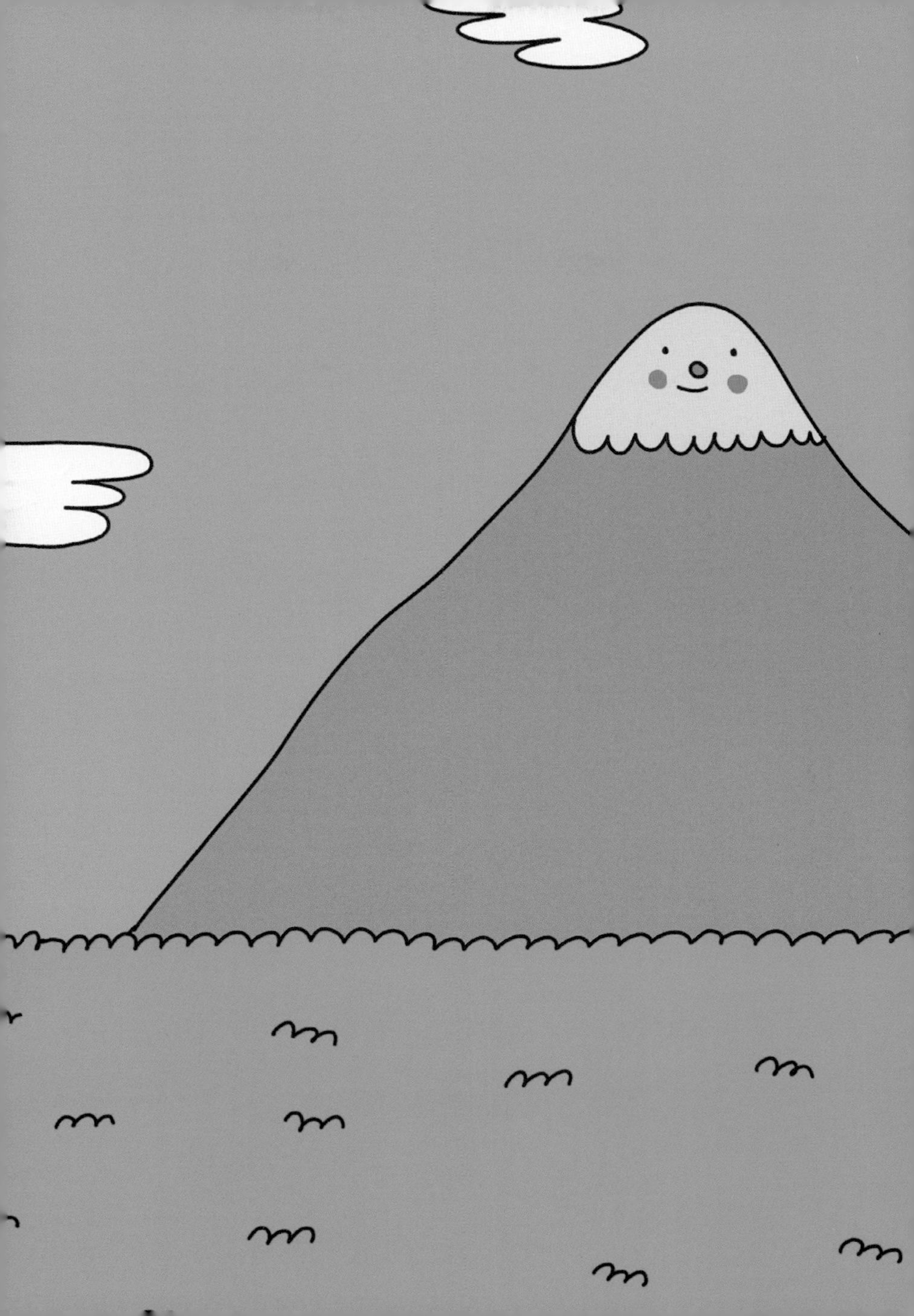

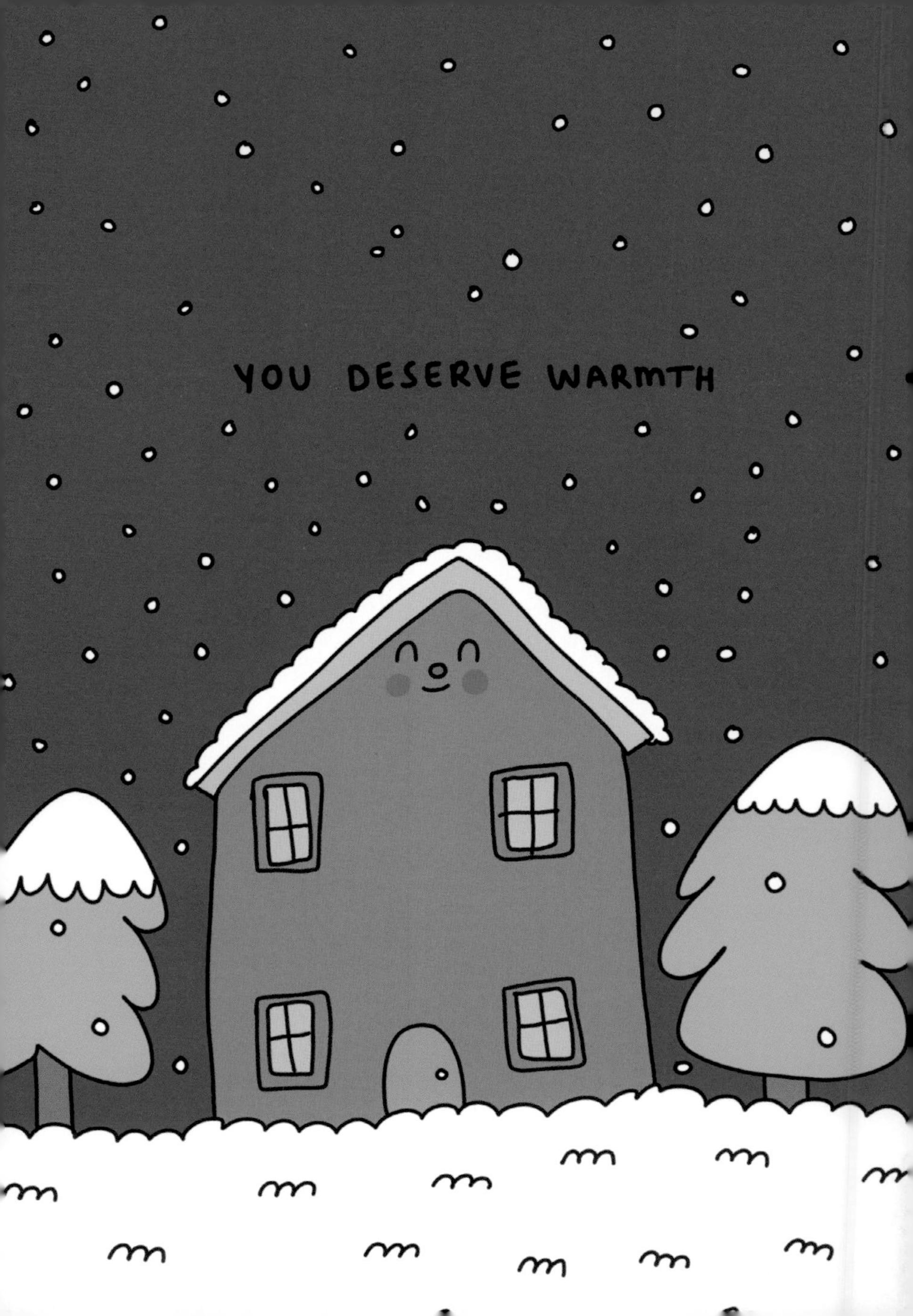
YOU DESERVE WARMTH

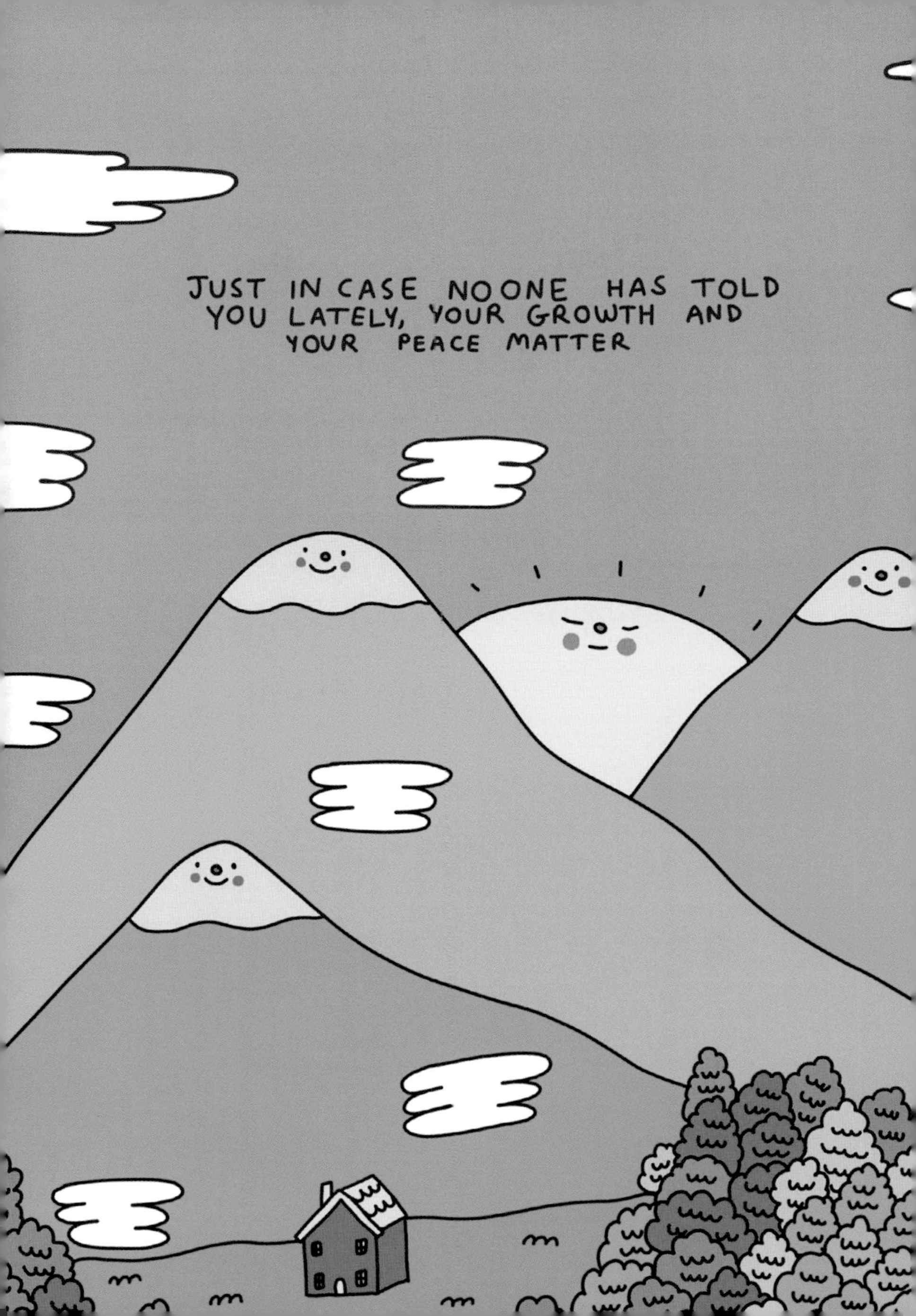
JUST IN CASE NOONE HAS TOLD YOU LATELY, YOUR GROWTH AND YOUR PEACE MATTER

You are easy to love.

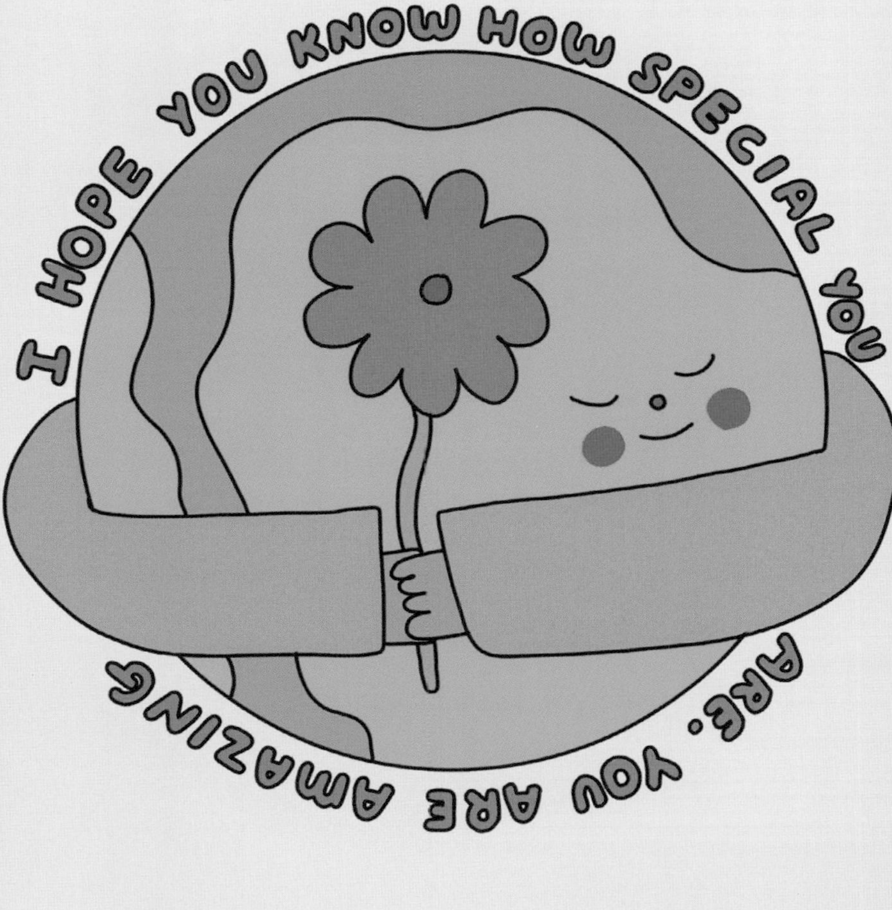
I HOPE YOU KNOW HOW SPECIAL YOU ARE. YOU ARE AMAZING

YOU MADE IT HERE THROUGH 100% OF YOUR BAD DAYS.
YOU DID THAT. SO REMEMBER TO BE GENTLE WITH YOURSELF.

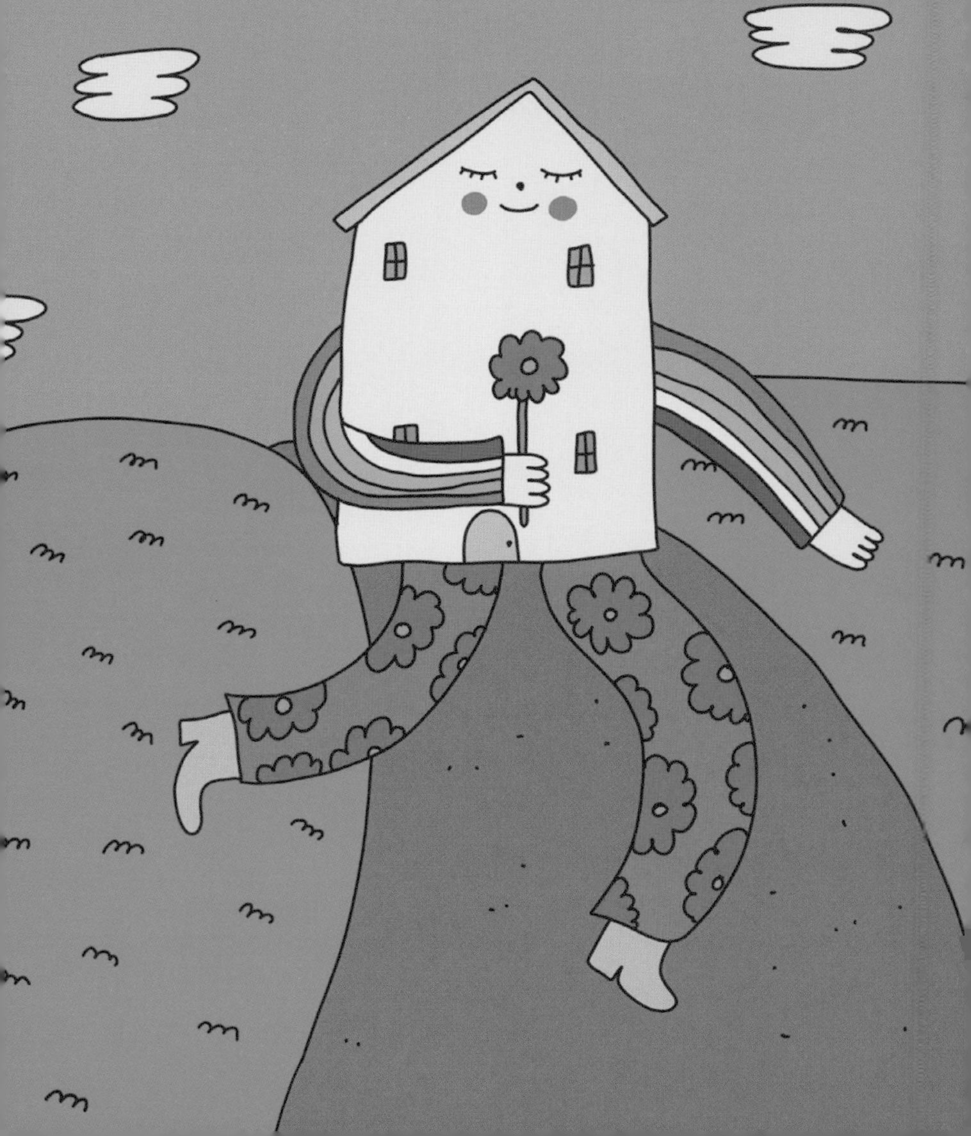

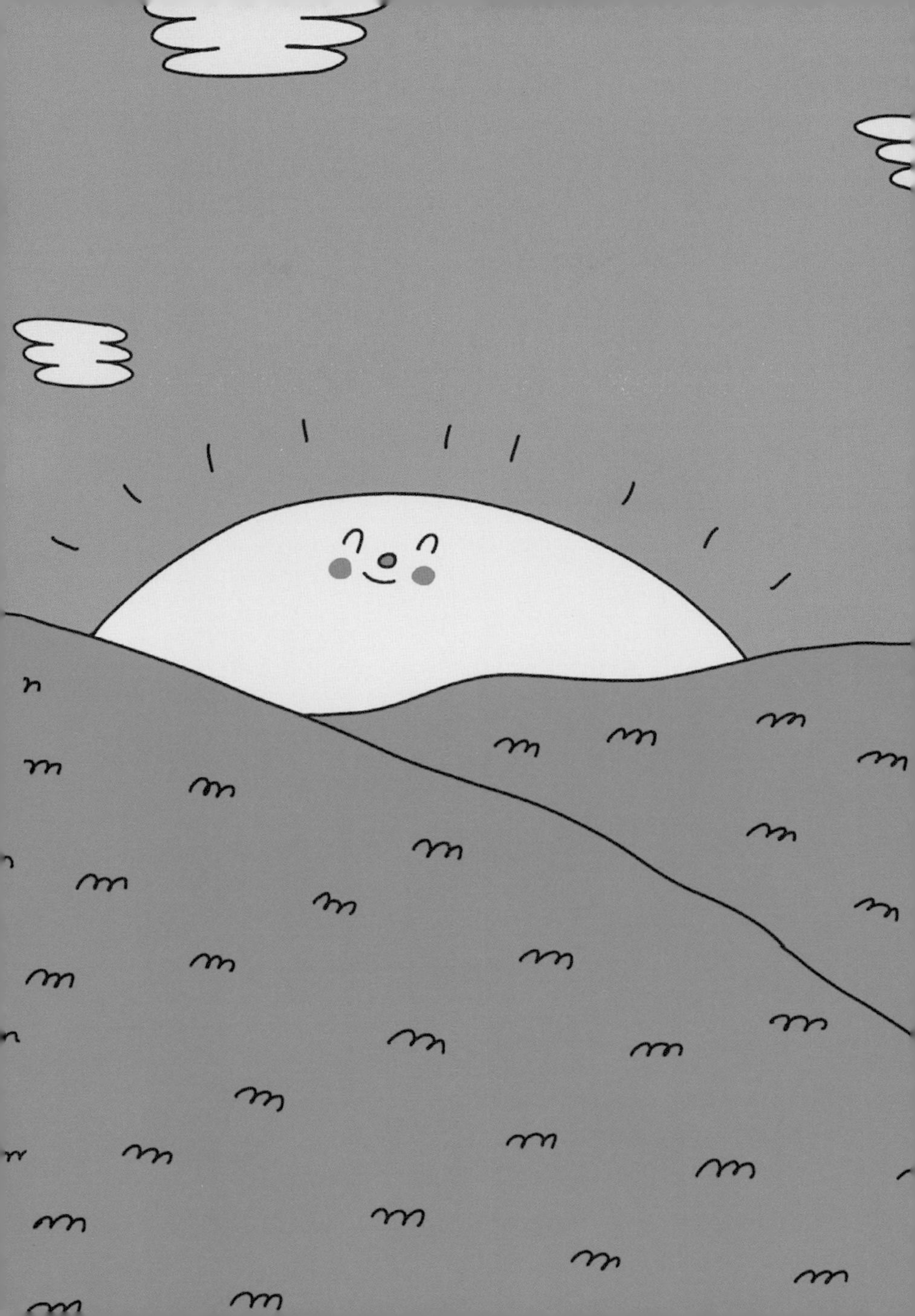

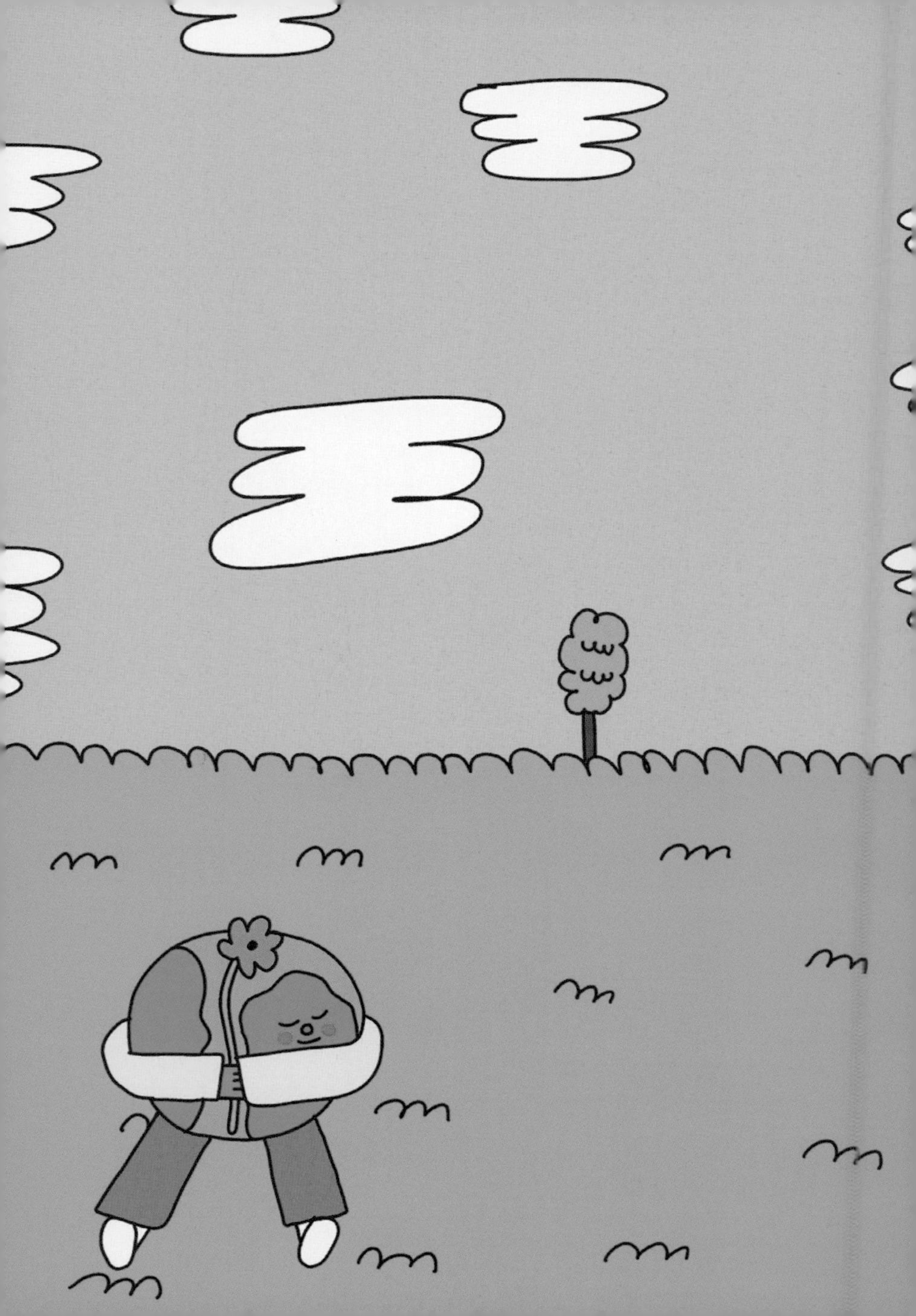

WOW - LOOK AT YOU GO! I'VE WATCHED YOU FALL DOWN AND YOU ALWAYS GET BACK UP AGAIN. I HOPE YOU KNOW HOW MUCH STRENGTH THAT TAKES! YOU ARE PROOF THAT THERE IS BRIGHTNESS IN THIS WORLD. EVEN WHEN EVERYTHING FEELS DARK.

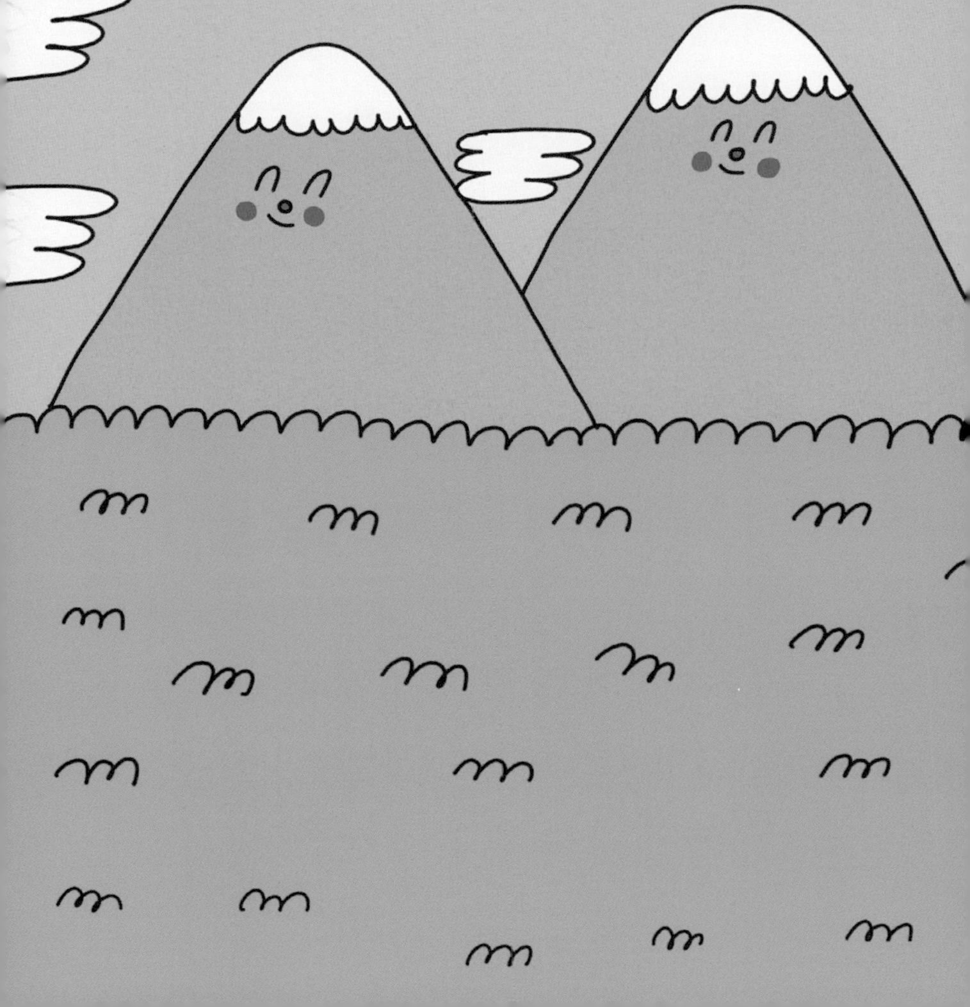

YOU DESERVE SOFTNESS. IT'S OK TO NEED YOUR LIFE TO BE CALM AND FULL OF LIGHT. YOU DESERVE IT ALL...

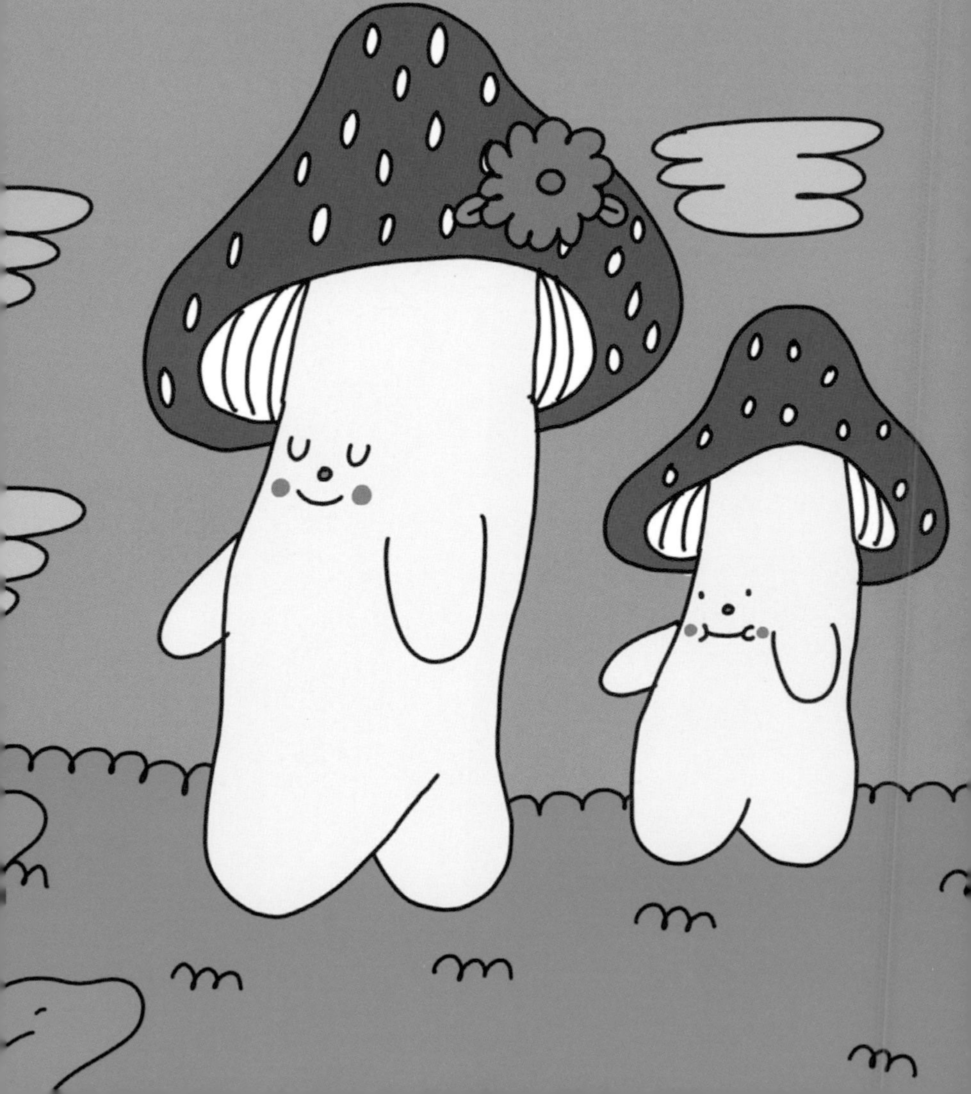

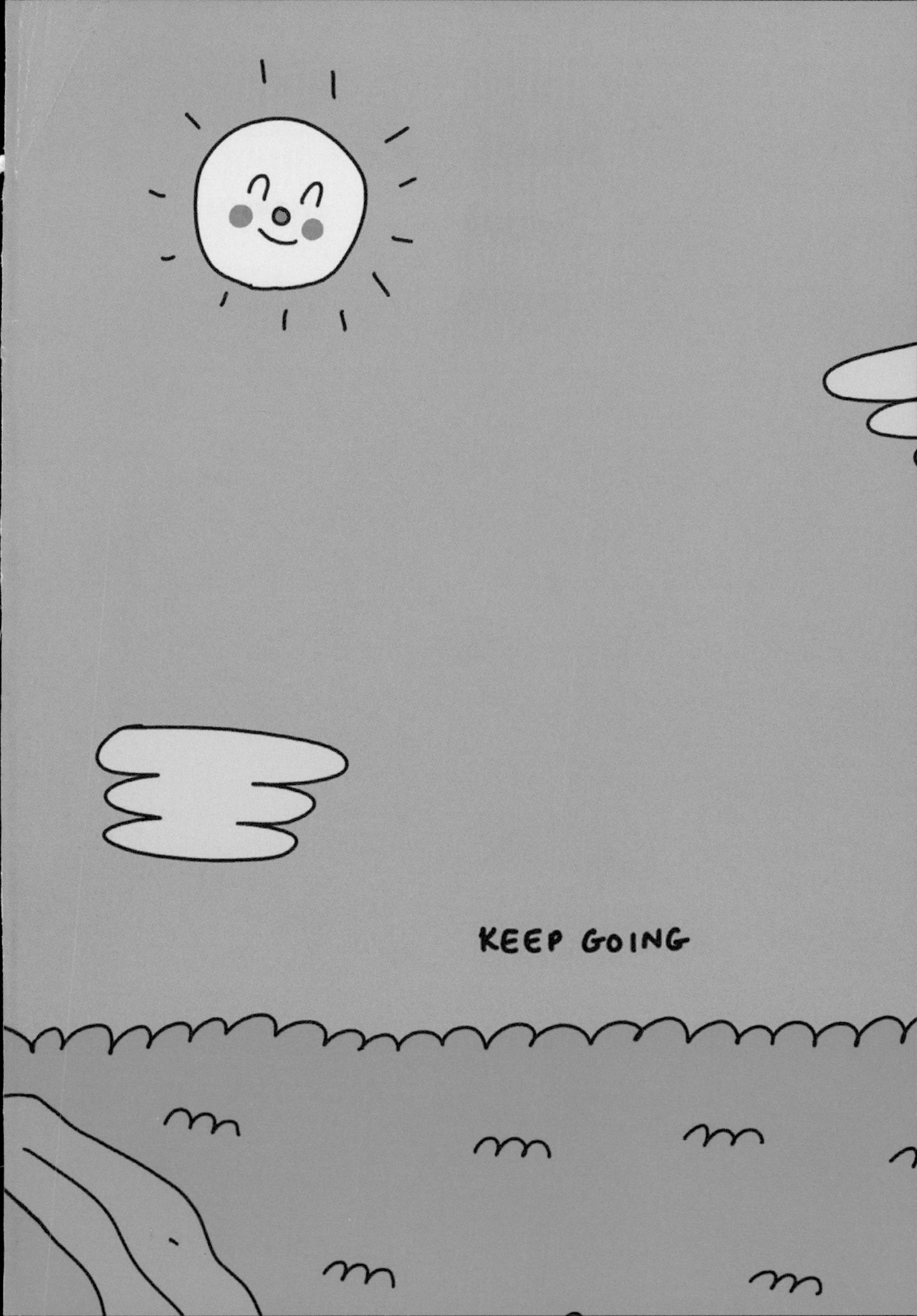
KEEP GOING